SWAP

MARKETING WITHOUT MONEY

THERESE TARLINTON

KMD
BOOKS

First published in Australia in 2022
by KMD Books
Waikiki, WA 6169

Edited by Tracy Regan

Typeset in Sabon LT Pro 11/15pt

A catalogue record for this
work is available from the
National Library of Australia

National Library of Australia Catalogue-in-Publication data:

SWAP: Marketing Without Money/Therese Tarlinton

ISBN:
978-0-6454076-0-0
(Paperback)

ISBN:
978-0-6453319-9-8
(Ebook)

To the men who support me every day and make me strive for better

Derek, Will and Luke

And the sisters I chose myself who are there for the triumphs, the struggles, and always ready with cocktails

Toni, Sarah, Lea, Viki, Mel and Sue

INTRODUCTION

In our post-pandemic world, small businesses are doing it tougher than ever before. Brands need to find a way of leveraging their assets and form partnerships with companies to create products and services their mutual customers value, while helping each other grow in the process. Therese Tarlinton used this strategy to build a global manufacturing company in her twenties, after partnering with Jeep, United Colors of Benetton and Sesame Street.

After twenty years of navigating and securing international licensing deals, TV product placement through to content swaps, Therese can guarantee that marketing partnerships are the creative way to do more with less. She now works for the big brands, collaborating with The Block, Three Birds Renovation, and identities including Shelley Craft to secure her brands have a constant stream of content, credibility and sales.

SWAP was written to assist brands with a step-by-step process to understand their value, find the right partners, collaborate on deals and become a sought-after brand by over-delivering on their customers' expectations.

CONTENTS

Chapter 1
PARTNERSHIPS ARE THE SECRET SAUCE IN MARKETING

'Big business shouldn't be afraid to say that they don't have all the answers, and they really must recognise that small businesses can play a big part in helping develop new ways to make business better.' – **Richard Branson**

In the late 1990s when I started out in marketing, there was a huge divide between big and small businesses. Corporates had layers of management, rules to follow and bulging budgets to spend. Media was elusive and coveted; you paid to get your brand in front of your customers. Times have changed, and these days, small brands have the same opportunities as the big corporates, but they need each other more than ever.

In the early 2000s, I burst out of my corporate uniform and mindset and created my own company. I went from a startup idea to a million dollars in turnover in my first year by using strategic marketing partnerships. Fast-forward to 2022 and partnerships are now being used by thousands of brands but are a little misunderstood. It's much more than an Instagrammer taking your product and posting a story

1

with it. I want to show you how successful partnerships *can take your fifteen seconds of fame and turn it into years of profitability.*

Partnerships are an important element in your marketing strategy

In our post-pandemic world, small businesses need to use every asset they have to survive and grow. It is when they realise their true value and join forces in collaboration with another brand where they can reach a new audience, elevate their brand and grow their sales. Brand collaborations provide an incredible advantage to those who invest and go down deep into strategic marketing partnerships. Businesses often just dip their toe in the water and play it safe with their partnership strategy but really need to be thinking more innovatively. They need to form alliances to improve their offering as well as their chances of success.

With a tight economy and brands fighting to survive, now is the time to start looking at opportunities partnering with other companies. If you don't, you risk exhausting all your marketing budget, never achieving the sales you need to stay in business.

Most entrepreneurs have a great a business idea, quit their day job and borrow money to get started. And the last thing anyone wants is to return to their old life with a deflated ego and an empty bank account.

Over the last twenty years, every time I struggled financially, it was when I tried to go it alone. Partnerships have rescued me every single time, whether that was a partnership to create a new product, a marketing campaign to reach a new audience, joining forces to enhance my credibility or developing a new distribution line with another brand.

A marketing partnership is a 100% proven method to scale your business and will get you in front of thousands of your dream customers. This book will help to turn you into a partner that other businesses want to work with. I have a proven framework and it takes you through three phases: **attract, act** and **advance**. I want to teach you how to find the right partners and make yourself attractive to them. I want you to be thinking in ways that will add value to your partnerships and customers, where you are gaining their trust while both achieving your goals. You will be able to show a return on investment and put yourself in a position where you can find the next partnership deal, and the next, enabling you to grow and scale your business.

I AM A LIVING EXAMPLE OF HOW

Let me show you how I discovered this.

I had a successful career in marketing with the big brands, but I was looking for a way to create a business of my own. I found a small company on the market for sale that interested me, but after some negotiation, we agreed to help each other. I would help her launch her brand in America, and she would teach me the highs and lows of owning a small business. While on a trip to Boston I saw a branded baby stroller and a light bulb went off in my head! Having worked in branding for several global companies, I thought a branded stroller might be a good fit for the Australian market. I met with the manufacturer who was also at the same baby expo, and they agreed to provide me with a few samples.

On my return to Australia, I researched the products, the price points, the distribution model, the retailer's ranges and the marketing to mothers. I recognised a gap in the nursery industry for a branded stroller that appealed to the parents instead of the child. At that stage, the only brands appearing on strollers were Elmo, Cookie Monster and Mickey Mouse. If you were a young professional couple, your choices were cute or functional; the only international brands in Australia were Maclaren and Peg Perego.

I shared a booth at a baby expo and showed the stroller to the thousands of expectant parents to see if there was an appetite for the product. That booth literally catapulted me into my own business. I got pre-orders from over a hundred parents, which demonstrated there was a real demand for that type of stroller at that price in the market. The demand illustrated to my husband it was a calculated risk and we got a personal bank loan for $120,000. Those pre-orders also demonstrated to my first retailers to take a chance and stock the product.

I had a couple of Jeep baby strollers to show retailers and decided to meet with the public relations manager for Jeep in Australia. I spoke enthusiastically about my big idea to bring their strollers to Australia because they had huge, inflatable all-terrain wheels and there were no lifestyle branded baby products in Australia at the time. The PR manager was pregnant and unbeknownst to me, I created my first partnership when she said, 'You know what? I'll tell your story if I can have all of these products. I love them.' She crafted my media releases and secured editorials in every magazine and newspaper across Australia from the *Financial Review* to all the baby magazines. That was my first glimpse into marketing collaborations where you exchange value with another party and it's not necessarily a cash deal.

That first partnership attracted my first big retailer. I went to Target to meet with the nursery buyer, and on the day, the CEO walked past the room. He put his head in the door and told the buyer he was going to be instore next week and wanted to see my product on the floor! He had seen the strollers in the newspapers and wanted Target to be the first with the brand.

The fact we were stocked in Target, gave other retailers

the confidence to stock the brand, and the national exposure got me into my next partnership. As my customers were pregnant women and mothers of newborns, Huggies nappies reached out through their promotional agency and said, 'We've got an idea and we want to give away a Jeep to a mother and baby.' I provided Huggies with a few strollers as prizes and the image of my stroller would be on the nappy boxes and advertising flyers in every Coles supermarket across the country for three months.

That was a very big first year of business! After each marketing collaboration I kept the images, flyers and advertising to show to my next potential partner. This success helped me to secure my next brand – partnering with Sesame Street. That then gave me credibility for my next licensing partnership out of Europe with United Colors of Benetton. They didn't have a range of strollers, cots or highchairs but I knew they had partners creating luggage and school stationery. I figured I had nothing to lose, so I flew to Italy and spoke about my idea to create a range for European mothers.

They loved the idea! So much so, they put the idea out to tender with other businesses. I was competing against huge global giants in the industry and I was just a young mum with four staff in Sydney. I nearly didn't put in a submission as I assumed I had no chance of winning, but decided no matter what the outcome was, I would go down swinging. My story was a fashionable mother's perspective, a passionate maker's dedication to the brand values and characteristics, and a launch strategy that was brave and bold. AND I WON! The experience taught me that there are manufacturers and then there are marketers who make products. People buy into the story, the feeling, the belief and the vision. The United Colors of Benetton baby products range was going to be an investment for parents, but the payoff was there. Unlike commodity goods, which don't need vision, just the lowest price, this would be a product range customers *wanted* to buy.

Those licensing partnerships created momentum for me to expand globally and set up distribution partners in different countries. My first was in New Zealand, then South Africa, which got me into England, and then Spain and Germany.

I was a young woman going up against the older, established, stately brands in the industry. It was a different proposition for someone like me to be within that manufacturing industry, but I was able to gain brand trust. I knew about branding. I knew I had to get the trust of not only the parents who wanted the product, but also the trust of the retailers who wanted to stock it. By using partnerships, I was able to borrow the credibility of big brands like Jeep and United Colors of Benetton to leverage my business across a retailer and targeted audience which delivered sales that kept growing year after year.

When I started out I had almost no money for marketing, but between the trade show and setting up distributors, it was only a couple of years where money was tight. I was doubling my sales each year, as I was actively seeking new partnerships. I saw partnerships as a third-party endorsement by a brand my customers trusted. The success of the business took me into another sphere, where the government put me on an accelerated growth program and gave me some funding.

I want to show you that while you might think that creating marketing partnership is hard, like lots of entrepreneurs, I was just showing up and looking for every opportunity. I was open-minded to using partnerships as a strategy to grow, scale and get further introductions. This was before social media appeared and was all done in a very frugal way. Partnerships were the key to how I created a global business.

Then I sold the company and took partnerships into corporate

The company grew to a point where I would need to be in Europe for six months of the year. I had two small children, one starting school, and I decided it was time to let someone else take the company to the next level.

What I had learnt about partnerships I wanted to take to the big brands. I joined a large Australian Stock Exchange (ASX) listed ecommerce group who were growing fast. I was able to engage ambassadors to create content and help charities get the funds they needed to do great work.

My favourite was partnering with the McGrath Foundation, who help breast cancer sufferers. Created by the late Jane McGrath – the wife of Glen McGrath, the captain of the Australian cricket team – they provide patients with a personal nurse during treatment. I teamed them up with a bespoke creator of pink diamond jewellery who had experienced breast cancer in their family. The charity auction was able to harness the traffic of the site and encourage people to bid at auction on the pink diamonds, raising over $112,000 for the charity. I then repeated this for many charities using sought-after memorabilia like a Red Bull racing suit, ARL winners' jerseys and limited-release bottles of wine.

Over the following years I helped service-based brands in software, real estate property development and the leading candle manufacturer, to use partnerships to create marketing campaigns, elevating their brands and reaching new audiences.

Open your mind to the possibilities

Having a partnership mindset will open possibilities for amazing benefits for both you and your customers. I am going to take you through the steps on how to create opportunities for partnerships in your business. There is a proven process that will help you attract partners, establish your brand and support your business growth. I want to give you the knowledge and confidence required to build partnerships. Adapt your marketing strategy to include strategic collaborations and your brand will be discovered. You can stop relying on Facebook ads to get in front of your ideal customers.

Developing partnerships is an age-old marketing technique. Remember the Nike Air Jordan sneakers? That was a brilliant collaboration between elite sportsperson Michael Jordan and leading footwear brand, Nike. The sneakers were released in 1985, and today, those original-style sneakers are selling for more than $10,000. They are a collectors' piece now, but in their day they were a symbol of status for the people who owned them. Or think of the McDonald's Happy Meal and the toy in it. As a kid, I would constantly pester my mother to have McDonald's so I could get the toy in the meal. Partnerships are a reliable source of marketing credibility and have been for many years.

American Express released a study in 2017 showing that half of the businesses using their credit services do not collaborate with other businesses. However, businesses that were highly collaborative had an average growth projection of 17% over the next twelve months and 64% of those businesses who were highly collaborative also grew their whole business within that twelve-month period. Part of the reason why this works is that collaboration is seen as more trustworthy than advertising.

The American Express Collaboration Index explored the question, does the investment made in collaboration generate a worthy return? Unequivocally the answer was YES. The research revealed mid sizes and small businesses achieved an return on their investment faster than they expected. The ROI within six months took the form of increased sales, reduction in costs or both. For large brands with CFO's,

ROI is the key question they ask, and this data shows the strong performance of collaboration investment made to provide a compelling case for all organisations to place an even greater emphasis on partnerships.

Some of the most successful collaborative businesses shared their insights into how they successfully collaborate. They concluded they keys to a successful collaboration were:

1. Establish a clear vision and shared values,
2. Align systems and processes.
3. Measure the return.
4. Think laterally about collaboration.

	Low/ Un-collaborative	Moderately Collaborative	Highly Collaborative
Percentage of businesses	48%	32%	20%
Average number of collaboration partnerships	1.7	2.3	5.5
Annual investment in collaboration	$13,514	$25,533	$45,598
ROI (increase in sales / reduction in costs	0.9	1.9	1.2
Average number of years collaborating	1.5	5	4
Proportion collaborating with businesses overseas	10%	18%	30%
Experienced revenue growth in the past 12 months	26%	54%	64%
Average revenue growth projected for coming 12 months	5%	7%	17%
New collaborations in the past 12 months	0.2	1.2	3

Source: American Express Collaboration Index

Dealing with the big brands

You might think that partnerships and collaborations are only for the big brands, but you would be wrong. You only know about those because you recognise their names. Every day, many small businesses are in partnerships. Think of your local primary school and how they promote the sign-up day for the rugby club at the local oval, or the real estate agent who posts on Instagram about where he is getting his coffee. A partnership can be a naturally aligned relationship, like when the electrician recommends a local plumber to collaborate with. This is a simple way of expanding your audience by having great relationships with other companies who will quote your name.

Partnerships do not need to be a formal, written deal. They can be flexible and casual, but the important thing is, they need to be reciprocal. Give as much as you are get. You need to be in a deal where both businesses feel happy and secure, and moving forward with your mutual customers or community benefitting.

Big brands are consistently approached for sponsorship deals where you pay to be part of something. Not many brands think to approach them about marketing collaborations. When I have received emails about a project, it is usually just asking for 'free stuff' with no offer of value in return. Large brands are not charities any more than small brands are. They exist to make a profit, with listed companies needing to report to shareholders.

SO, WHAT ARE BRAND COLLABORATIONS AND PARTNERSHIPS?

There are so many different styles of marketing collaborations and partnerships. Those we are all familiar with tend to be what we see on social media. These can be a competition or hashtag challenge and are small ways you can create a partnership that is quick and cost-effective.

But there are so many creative ways you can work with other brands. I want to open your mind to all the possibilities. It could be a digital, product or an experience partnership.

Partnership marketing is one of the fastest growing marketing strategies because it's about collaborating with other businesses to create campaigns that benefit both parties and always has the customer in mind. It is mutually beneficial for both the parties, as well as the customer.

Most small business owners don't think they have the knowledge or confidence to contact another company and ask to work together. This book will give you the road map and the tools so you won't need to be confident. You will have the recipe and you can follow it to find success.

What can partnerships do for your brand?

BRAND

- Increase your personal profile as a credible voice or authority.
- Elevate your brand in your customers' minds.
- Attract investors' attention.
- Win new retailers, stockists or distributors.
- Attract media attention and buzz.
- Grow your business network.

ASSETS

- Increase web traffic or foot traffic.
- Grow your database of customers or leads.
- Increase your social following.
- Reach a new audience without advertising.
- Increase the content you have to share with customers.
- Enhance your SEO, backlinks and customer journey mapping.
- Gain new business contacts to assist your infrastructure.

SALES

- Increase your sales to new customers.
- Re-engage dormant customers in your database.
- Add a new revenue stream to your business.
- Add new stockists, affiliates or advocates.
- Increase your average cart size.
- Reduce your price tension allowing you to charge more.

In this book, we are going to cover a SIX-step RECIPE:

RECIPE
For powerful partnerships

R **Rediscover**
Know your business worth and assets to leverage

E **Evaluate**
The objectives you want to achieve

C **Connect**
Find the right partners and explore possibilities

I **Implement**
Do the deal and over deliver on their expectations

P **Position**
Extend your reach to industry, stockists and media

E **Evolve**
Demonstrate the success and build advocates

SNAPSHOT

Having a partnership mindset has opened so many opportunities in my career. Partnerships are just one marketing lever you can pull to expose your brand to an audience of your ideal customers. After reading this chapter, I hope you feel it is worth pursuing.

The main barrier is simply starting. The first partnership is the hardest to get from a confidence point of view, but once you start making connections and you have a plan in place, companies will be attracted to you. You'll be a pro in no time!

In the next chapter we are going to dive into the different types of partnerships, and how you can extract value from them. You will understand when to get an event partner or do a digital campaign, versus a brand placement on TV. It comes down to what the aim is for your business.

It is the biggest chapter where you will gain the greatest amount of *gold*. Think of it as learning how a magician does their tricks. Once you know, you are one step ahead of the pack.

Chapter 2
DIFFERENT TYPES OF PARTNERSHIPS

The real marketing term is strategic partnerships, but since the advent of digital marketing and the accelerated pace we are now living in, the trendy term is brand collaborations. Throughout this book, I will use both terms as they are interchangeable. But what are they? In essence, it is when two complementary businesses team up on a clever marketing initiative, using their existing assets to create something the customer will value, while helping each other grow through clever cross-promotion.

There are many different types of possible partnerships to achieve your goals for your brand. We will look at what other savvy companies are doing, so you can squeeze every drop out of your collaboration and know what to ask for.

THE KEY DIFFERENCES BETWEEN PARTNERSHIPS AND INFLUENCER MARKETING

Partnerships are not the same as influencer marketing. Influencer marketing is where you pay someone with a profile to deliver your message to their audience and a company usually deals with an individual person who has a strong following. Partnerships, on the other hand, are brand to brand, meaning companies deal with other companies. Let me explain how they differ:

1. Businesses have more assets than influencers which can be used to convey your joint message. You are leveraging multiple marketing channels as most businesses have social, website, stores, email lists, LinkedIn, event audiences, product development and retail outlets or even showrooms. Plus, they have professional industry credibility. There are many more promotional channels available through using businesses as partners.
2. In a partnership, you are leveraging all the channels of communication and distribution, rather than paying an influencer a fee to say things about your product. You are using the assets you have built in your business to gain more exposure, providing a higher value offer to your audiences.
3. Long-term relationships often form with authentic businesspeople. Those people talk to their network and your exposure grows. I always ask other companies their opinion on working with a particular brand.

Brand collaborations are a brilliant way to leverage the assets you have in your company, to reach potential new customers. You both agree to contribute to build something for the customer or a promotion where you can cross-promote each other's business. It's smart marketing where you leverage assets other than cash, so little or no money changes hands. You need to align your goal to the type of partnership that will allow both companies to benefit. It's nice having cool business friends, but if you don't get the success you intended from the deal, you would have been better off having cocktails with them instead.

When to use influencer marketing

Fashion brands, cosmetics, candles and even homewares manufacturers release new products for Christmas and Mother's Day and limited editions, or you may have seasonal products around a sporting season, weather change or even when produce is in season. When you have a product that needs a lot of attention and moves quickly, influencers are a fantastic option. Using the widespread industry practice of paying influencers who create content and share this with their audience to power a movement for retailers to sell through the stock quickly is not unusual.

Influencer charges vary but for a set fee, plus gifting them the products, they create a targeted content piece to tell their audience about a product. This can also be a service, an event or a sale. Critically, the influencer decides how they are going to deliver the message and the words they use are their own. They do this as their authentic voice is why people follow them on social media and why companies want to work with them. It sounds less like an ad and more like a conversation between friends, which is why this delivers the best cut through. It is a brilliant way to also assess their suitability to become an ambassador for your brand.

A partnership is very different, as usually a payment is not exchanged and multiple messages and mediums are used during the campaign.

The Block is an Australian reality renovation show aired on the Nine Network four nights each week, for twelve weeks. They recruit five couples who must design, build and decorate one room every week. Each Sunday night they 'reveal' their room and one of the couples wins $10,000 in cash for that week to use in their house renovation. At the end of the series, each house is auctioned, and the contestants' prize money is the difference between the reserve set by the show and the final selling price. Year after year, many of the couples walk away with several hundred thousand dollars, which in most instances, changes their lives. The clever contestants use their new profile to become ambassadors for other brands.

Many manufacturers have a partnership with *The Block* TV series, while others become a sponsor, which also secures advertising in the commercials around the program. CSR manufactures building products including bricks, roof tiles, cladding, insulation and plasterboard – all the products you need to build a home. Colorbond roofing, Beaumont Tiles, Beacon Lighting, Kinsman Kitchens and Freedom furniture are also suppliers with partnerships.

CSR have been an avid supporter of this program since its very first season and have provided the products to the production company under a collaboration deal agreement. Like all the other suppliers to the show, CSR receives mentions of their products on TV by the contestants, images on-screen of their products being installed plus room reveal product details on *The Block* website with links to the CSR website.

The images of *The Block* homes when finished are used extensively in the product marketing of all these supplier brands, as they show the products in real life. In this style of partnership, you can see that *The Block* receives all the products they need to build, saving them over a million dollars in product costs, and suppliers like CSR receive visibility on a TV broadcast show in return.

DIFFERENT TYPES OF PARTNERSHIPS YOU CAN EXPLORE

Partnership
Collaboration Types

Experiences

Product   Digital

1. **Digital partnerships** centre on creating a product or promotion that is shared with your audience to increase your brand awareness and get your ideal customers clicking to find out more on your digital channels.
2. **Product partnerships** are based on what you sell every day and what your key identifying factor is plus your skill. It could also be a combination of the product and the distribution channel where you get to introduce your product to another audience.
3. **Experience partnerships** can be an event or location share, or where people come to have a physical experience in person with others along with the brands.

DIGITAL PARTNERSHIPS

Digital partnerships allow low-cost products and promotions to be developed to reach new audiences. The first collaboration that usually comes to mind are competitions and giveaways with brands who are aligned or have similar-sized audiences, so they can leverage each other's community. The key is to keep it selective and authentic, otherwise people follow to enter and then unfollow as soon as they don't win. This type of collaboration could include a hashtag challenge such as 'choose which house you'd want to live in', or 'tell us in twenty-five words or less who you'd want to take on a weekend away'. The aim is to get the audience of another account to follow you and then grow to love your brand. Social media collaborations are the quickest way to dip your toe in the partnership water.

Gyprock partnered with Soul Home to build their new holiday property, The Pause, on the South Coast of Sydney. Part of the deal was a three-night stay giveaway. This was an Instagram competition where homeowners had to follow @gyprockliving and @thepauseau to win. With these styles of collaborations, it is not unusual to increase your following by thousands during the promotional period.

Here are some other examples:

- Being a guest on a podcast.
- Teaming up to deliver a webinar with other brands.
- Creating a downloadable available on a website other than your own.
- Delivering a course to teach a skill, for a service or how to use a product.
- Creating content, whether it's a video or article that talks about both brands.
- Creating images where both brands are represented e.g. a dress with shoes.
- Doing a social media post that includes another brand
- Recommending another brand in your electronic direct mail (EDM).

STEPS TO A GREAT DIGITAL COLLABORATION

1. Define your goal – what do you want to get out of the collaboration?

   If your goal is to increase your Instagram following, then consider what action you will take with your new followers once you get them. For example, you could send them a direct message (DM) with a link to a video on your website or a code that offers them a discount on your products.
2. Know your value. What is a fair trade with your partner?

   If your audience size is smaller or less engaged than your partner's audience, you can add value to the deal by doing a video about the competition or sharing it on LinkedIn.
3. Have an engaging idea and execute it well.

   The idea needs to be engaging for your audience but you both need to achieve your objectives. Think about

HelloFresh and Jimmy Brings – a win-win value exchange. The customer is interested in bringing food and wine to their home.

4. Make sure it makes sense and does not look too staged.

You should have similar target markets or demographics, or complimentary industry spaces so the collaboration makes sense, for example, a vet and a dog walker, or a stylist and a clothing brand. I often get emails from a known Linkedin expert who recommends others who teach strategies to grow on other channels like webinars, TikTok and guest podcasts.

5. Ensure you leverage beyond social media.

Think about all the marketing channels in your eco-system – email list, email signature, podcast, LinkedIn, Facebook live, retail stores, orders in boxes. It's important to have an agreed and mutually promoted plan, but you can always do more than you have committed to doing.

Competitions are a simple first step into collaborations. Offer up something of value or contribute to a group campaign and ask your audience to follow another company. It is easy to do and creates a different conversation with your audience.

My favourite types of digital collaborations are when you create something of value. Try-a-little-before-you-buy is a time-tested way to gain trust with customers before you get them to buy your full product.

Create content together so it feels like inside knowledge

If you have a digital service you could offer a course, or a downloadable magazine or research paper. *The top five secrets of interior designers* will always be appealing and will give your partners something of value to offer their clients. It's even better if it's tailored to both of you.

TileCloud, an online bathroom and kitchen tile retailer, have clients with great taste who produce fantastic images of finished rooms using their tiles. An image of a single tile sitting in a box isn't as appealing as a stunning new bathroom. Doing a collaboration where you exchange a product for a digital asset, like images and posts, is a great win for both parties and the customer gets to experience the product in a different way.

If CSR were to collaborate with TileCloud, they would create a booklet on *The five things you need to do before your tiles go on – tradies secrets edition.* It would talk about underfloor heating, insulation between bedrooms so the toilet flushing doesn't wake you up, inline fans that push air outside instead of noisy ones that sound like a plane taking off, waterproof plasterboard so you don't get black spots on your ceiling, and power points in your drawers.

Both brands would be able to show leadership in their areas to improve the brand trust, position against their competitors and have an asset they can use long-term as a lead magnet to attract renovators to each website.

Repurpose your content so it's customised for their audience

What do your customers do before they come to see you? Accountant before financial planner. Real estate agent before architect. Architect before builder. Builder before landscaper. There are lots of people you could have a referral-style relationship with already and create some digital assets to help with your lead generation.

Think about the content you already have that could be repurposed to include their product or the service they offer. Writing an article that has an assortment of brands or tips is more engaging than a piece that is exclusively about one brand, as it looks like an ad.

Giveaways that cost you nothing

1. A referral program where businesses could get $50 worth of Google Ads for free. (Agencies are given complimentary advertising budgets for no cost to encourage clients to start advertising all the time, so it does not cost them a thing.)
2. If you are a financial planner, offer a cheat sheet on *The top five deductions you should be claiming right now.* At the bottom, offer a one-hour discovery session with a senior planner, worth $300.
3. A big bucket of digital goodies like Instagram frames, Canva templates or worksheets – everyone likes a freebie.

Your network can be your asset

Lastly, there are ways you can share what others need. If your partner has a podcast, webinar or YouTube series, they will need people to interview. Think of something you could offer them that they need. Offering a partner something they cannot get, but that you have, is liquid gold.

So, I Quit My Day Job is one of my favourite podcasts. Cathrine Mahoney interviews people who have made the leap to start their own business. Imagine if I had a community group of business owners with great stories. Do you think she would like to come along and meet some of them?

She needs constant content and a steady stream of new talent. Some people won't be appropriate for her audience and others will chicken out, but she could connect with some talented people she's never heard of before.

Steps to uncover gold and potential brand partners

1. Make a list of the podcasts, videos, YouTube channels and webinars you are interested in partnering with. Find the five popular trends and create a message about that. Pitch it to the

podcast/YouTube producers to see if they will interview you or at least take your content and promote it on their channels.

2. Look at the frequently asked questions you get in your social DMs, comments and emails from your website. Could you pitch these questions to the partner and show you are the one with the answers?

3. Take a dive into the forums in your niche, e.g. for building and renovating, Reno School and Bunnings mums Facebook groups. See what questions they have relating to your product category or industry. You now have a list of content you could write and tag in those forums to share your knowledge.

4. Look at the types of videos being watched on YouTube about competitor products and see if you can create similar content. If being seen on camera makes you want to run for the hills or hide under a rock, there are other ways. You could create a video using a team shot and all the content is pictures and words with a voiceover using your voice, or another person recording it.

5. Look at what your partners are missing. I know I am always looking for video content. If I can impart one thing I know from twenty years of marketing it is this: if you can only create one piece of marketing from your budget, make it a video. From video, you can get stills to use as photos, strip audio to make a podcast, transcribe the audio and make it into a blog or media release, take highlights and put it on social media. There are so many possibilities.

YOUR PRODUCTS ARE YOUR BIGGEST ASSETS AND YOUR GREATEST CHANCE TO INCREASE YOUR SALES

If you are one of the lucky brands who have a physical product, you have an asset that can work for you in many ways.

Working with a partner who can introduce your products to their audience can be the best move you will ever make. You also have something else of value – the knowledge and contacts to take an idea into a product that sits on the shelf. Don't underestimate the years you've invested in that.

Product collaborations are all about driving sales, creating a buzz and attracting media attention. Your unknown product can become your next customer's regular purchase if your partner shares that they trust your brand and the product is worth buying.

Licensing a well-known brand

I created my first business by identifying that having a big brand on my product instantly made it more alluring and gave it greater 'stand-out' quality, as well as a better chance of selling in the stores. Licensing a brand is an official, legally binding investment that is guaranteed. It's a formal brand collaboration but is not just the domain of global companies. You can find a brand that will elevate your product and acquire the license.

Adidas and McDonald's launched a 'sauce pack' collaboration. It was a modern interpretation that included NBA players James Harden, Damian Lillard and Tracy McGrady who, alongside sneakers and a set of graphic tees, have a go-to item on the McDonald's menus – the sauce. They linked it by saying each player has their own secret sauce on the court and brings their own flavour to the game.

Frito-Lay partnered with Mad Engine to create a new lifestyle range of fashion accessories. New collections will feature Cheetos and Doritos branded comic characters and the clothes are targeted at a large, diverse customer base who enjoy the food.

Amsterdam-based Pop Trading Company are bringing classic character Miffy into the skateboarding world with a collaboration with Converse Jack Purcell Pro sneakers.

There are some giants in the licensing area you can explore, and the Joester Loria Group is one. They represent big names and put brands together. I signed a licensing deal with them for Australian territory for the Jeep license to manufacture strollers, highchairs and cots and I was in my twenties with only two staff in my company at that stage. It's possible!

I can't talk highly enough about licensing. This is how I fell in love with partnerships. A well-known brand opens doors to retail and connects with customers quickly. It is faster than trying to develop a brand by yourself, and the brand itself invests heavily to maintain its recall and position. Licensing means you guarantee the brand an amount each year from your sales, paid quarterly. The percentage can vary from 3% to 15%, depending on the brand, the category and the region. This is based on the net wholesale selling price, minus any discounts. However, this cost is often negated by the increased sales you receive by having a brand on your product that people recognise and connect with.

Think about the risk and the reward together. I would never have been able to walk into Target and get a national deal on the spot when I was in my twenties, had I made a stroller in China with an unrecognised brand. The brand got their attention and the manufacturer who made products for Walmart gave them assurance that it was a viable product with an increased chance of selling. This also gave Target something unique that other retailers didn't have.

Extend your product into different categories

Think widely about the opportunity to collaborate and create a new product to appeal to your target customers in a different way. When you do this, you are creating new sales channels for your product.

Lara Scolari is a brilliant abstract artist who uses acrylics and oil paints to create her unique artworks. She is loved by interior designers around the country and her artworks take three months to create each piece. Lara decided to be commercial about her art. When she realised that commercial customers, like restaurants, loved her art but wanted it to be bigger, she partnered with Luxe Walls, a manufacturer who create removable wallpaper. She also has a deal with Designer Rugs who made her artwork into rugs or huge carpets; one of which sits in Parliament House in Canberra. She has also collaborated with a local sculpture artist where they created a theme which both artists followed in their mediums, before having a joint gallery exhibition inviting both their followers.

Think of what you do and go sideways

The opportunity might be within your own industry and could even be a competitor in some respects. Teaming up can sometimes be the most creative resolution for both partners to win.

Gelato Messina have stores in high-traffic suburbs of Sydney and are known for creating brilliant combinations of delicious gelato flavours. They did a deal with Peters Ice Cream for limited edition Drumstick cones – the ones your parents love – which saw them collaborate on flavours, enabling Peters to offer supermarket chains a way to attract a new demographic. This opened a new revenue chain for Gelato Messina but also gave them added credibility in that a huge company like Peters valued their product creation.

If you cannot think sideways, get your kids to do it. They are masters of innovation as they do not believe they have a bad idea. Here's some ideas to get you thinking:

- A candle and an artist for a Mother's Day range
- A Tim Tam flavoured cocktail for a new bar
- A Ferrari-branded steering wheel for Xbox to launch a new game
- A limited-edition wine featuring the Australian of the Year, with profits going to women's shelters.

For four months during the Sydney COVID-19 lockdown, I got OpenTable delivered. It's a meal delivery service where they provide all the ingredients for an inexpensive, delicious meal you cook for your family. When I opened the box, there was a flyer for Reading Eggs to trial for free. Reading Eggs is an online software program aimed at primary school children to allow them to learn reading and writing skills through play. For many parents homeschooling, they felt like they weren't helping their children enough while trying to juggle working from home, and this was a very nice collaboration to help the parent and the child navigate through this difficult period. Of course, it was a brilliant marketing idea, too.

Your product on a TV program

Having your product seen or used is also a great way to endorse the product and create trust. Seeing others use the product creates aspiration value. For over twenty years, I have been working with TV shows to get client's brands integrated into the programming. It started with *Better Homes and Gardens* in the nineties, *The Living Room* on Network 10, *Selling Houses Australia* and *Grand Designs* on Foxtel and the ever-popular, long-running renovation show *The Block*.

If you don't have a TV budget, then getting your product on the screen and seen by millions tastes sweet. It delivers the metrics that see your sales increase, assists your sales team to create a stronger value proposition for stockists and the credibility factor of appearing with recognised programs. It could be a program, a TV commercial or a locally produced series.

Having your homewares – be it pottery, cushions or lights – placed in an advertisement for a lounge company can still increase your brand awareness and extend your brand to a new audience. You can share this to your fans and retailers to illustrate that your brand was chosen as it aligns with the other brand.

Product placement is not only the domain of big brands. Could they be drinking your wine, pushing your stroller, wearing your clothes or sitting on your bespoke kitchen stools? When I manufactured the Jeep strollers, I was able to get it onto the highest-rating TV soap opera at the time, *Love My Way*, with well-known Australian actress Asher Keddie pushing it. I made sure I alerted my retailers, and they immediately ordered more stock for the anticipated demand. They relayed the story to persuade customers to buy the stroller and name drop its appearances at mothers' groups.

PR and advertising agencies are always filming TV commercials. Production companies are always creating shows and video content. Getting your product in front of executives is key. It could be clothing for the actors, your wine or gin placed on the kitchen bench or the tent in the back of an outdoor shot.

Ideas for product collaborations:

- Your knowledge of compliance, standards and safety in your industry to create your product.
- Industry contacts to manufacture the product, so you could make the product for another brand.
- Your logistics and warehousing insight to get products into national retailers.
- Digital assets you've built that attract an audience like videos using a branded product.
- Your showroom, your office, your warehouse as a stage for other brands.
- Your customer insights from their ordering and behaviour.
- Your brand trust with an audience giving you authority to speak about a complimentary product.
- High profile name of the leader of your business that people would love to interview.

AN EXPERIENCE GATHERING YOUR IDEAL CUSTOMERS TOGETHER BUILDS MEMORABLE BRANDS

Let's talk about the different types of in-person experiences. If you are going to create an event, think of all the companies needed to participate to bring the event to life – from catering, a location, audio visual, an MC and speaker, tools needed for a demonstration, decorations and the wine they serve. Small businesses need other cool collaborators so they can grow and learn from each other.

Get a group of people together and they will remember how they felt. It's an emotional and physical experience, where people can recall the details about what they heard, what they ate, who they spoke to and what they took away. As a marketing vehicle, an experience is the hands-down winner to getting customers to fall in love with your brand.

Where would your customers love to go? What do they love to see, hear or eat? How do they like to relax? Here are some ideas you could try for a memorable experience:

- Workshop – a fashion retailer with a physical store inviting people with a known stylist.
- Recurring meeting – a pub or restaurant offering space for a local community group.
- Event – launching a product and collaborating with a photographer.
- Training or educating your audience in a complimentary skill.
- A conference where you could speak to the audience.
- Offering your skill – photography, cooking, styling, music etc. to extend into a new audience.

VIP SHOWINGS WITH CELEBRITY CREDIBILITY

I was invited to Coco Republic when I studied interior design to see them launch a new collection. They had flown in Jonathan Adler, a designer from the USA. I was already a fan of Adler and that event turned me into a mega fan. Although I couldn't afford his furniture, I purchased some of his pottery and cushions. Coco Republic also have their own branded range of furniture, and this star power cascaded into their sales, with staff being overrun with orders on the night.

Turn digital into reality

You might be thinking, *I have an online company, so I don't need to get a heap of people in a room.* But, in fact, you need it more than a traditional retailer. It's so easy to swipe past on an app. Tinder had a very large presence at a Business Chicks weekend event that attracted thousands of professional businesswomen and small business owners. Having regular people talk about how a dating app took the stigma and scariness out of the product, while also legitimising it.

Are you a new online clothing store? At an event, you now become a real person with a name. People remember you and how you made them feel and can tell that story to their circle of influence.

Be part of a star line-up by using your real estate

Perhaps you're not ready to create an event yourself, but this is where you can dip your toe in the water and be involved in someone else's event. Use your location! If you have a retail space, restaurant, bar, boardroom, showroom – any physical location – then you have an asset people want. You also have something you can use yourself in a different way. Every in-person event needs a location. It is the central point, the most important element and can be the biggest drawcard in some ways.

Electrolux makes kitchen appliances. They have a super sexy showroom just outside the Sydney CBD, but it also feels a little intimidating. Three Birds Renovations create amazing homes that suburban mums swoon over – so white and dreamy, just delicious. They also have a following of over a million people on social media who are interested in building or renovating, so they created the Reno School – a course to teach you how to build your own dreamy white house.

Electrolux created a morning tea event where delicious food was made with their appliances and the Three Birds women came to speak to their adoring audience and answer their design questions. The chef created the food using Electrolux appliances, showing their products as appliances that are easy to use and can make you a better cook. Three Birds got to advocate a partner, meet their adoring fans and create a real-life connection to mega fans who would then buy their online course.

Think about everyone who would value what you have.

- Perhaps you are an artist with a beautiful gallery that could offer the space to an interior designer who wants to do a styling workshop and sell her new SketchUp course.
- Do you have a restaurant only open for lunch and dinner that could host a business breakfast? Introduce your venue to hundreds of locals who are always looking for somewhere new to dine.
- Imagine if MYOB had a boardroom with a harbour outlook. It would be in their interest to let out their space to another service company whose clients were small businesses so they could also talk about their software.
- If your space is more industrial than swish, you still have a space in demand. Keeping it real is an attraction to some. Fashion parades with an edge are the new look.
- If a venue is in the business of charging for the space, like a restaurant, then be realistic. They are not going to offer a space for free and have thousands of dollars of lost revenue.

There may be a situation where they could give a small space on a Tuesday night. If it's a new pub opening, they may not charge for the venue space, but attendees must pay for the food and drinks.

It's all about the deal delivering for everyone. If you approach a company with a venue and demonstrate the value for them, you have a better chance of success. They are not a charity and neither are you. Show up with a deal that is easy to say yes to.

Offer your name as the drawcard

Use your voice! Every event can use a drawcard. Often the speaker is the headline act. What could you teach or share that would entice others to sign up for the event? Getting your message across to a group creates an instant connection and a room full of advocates. I am not suggesting for a second your first gig is in front of 10,000 people. Start with your local community, a niche networking group, or an event with fifty people in a room who you could convert to customers in ten minutes of talking. Pretty good odds for a small business.

Sitecore is a huge international software company and has an annual conference where they invite both current and potential customers. They share insights and research that may help their customers grow, so it's worth attending. In 2019 they had Naomi Simpson, the founder of experience company RedBalloon, as the guest speaker. I've been a Naomi fan for more than a decade so I couldn't say yes quickly enough. I wasn't the only one, there were hundreds of people in the room.

Sitecore had a drawcard. Having Naomi as a guest speaker elevated the event with a buzz around iconic business RedBalloon being featured as a partner, instead of just a 'normal' software expo. RedBalloon uses Sitecore software, and in exchange for Naomi's appearance, they got a room full of people engaged with the new experiences they had just launched. Win-win.

The conference had an exhibition attached, full of other software companies and agencies who supported the software. Having Naomi on the ticket got more people to the venue. She then went into the exhibition area and offered attendees the chance of a photo with her, creating traffic for the exhibitors.

Many business owners are open to having a conversation onstage and sharing their story to inspire others. While there are people starting companies and becoming successful, there will always be others who are interested in how they did it or in working with them. Being brave and offering to do a ten-to-twenty-minute session on a panel or by yourself is an effective way to add a real personality to your brand and create a room full of advocates. We all love a *Rocky* underdog story.

Association is a good name-drop

The flip side of this same coin is that you've heard about a cool event with a great speaker, and you'd like to be part of it. There is everything to gain from contacting the organiser and offering your services.

Every event has a roll call of items needed to make it great. If you are a service-based business, this is where you can help. Aligning with events where your brand can be elevated is simply good business.

Would you hire a photographer who is a general freelancer, or a photographer who was the official photographer for the Sitecore conference? Partnerships can be used for credibility for your next job. Every time I am approached by a creative, digital or service-based agency with a pitch, the staple element in every presentation is a slide full of company logos of the brands they have worked with. Working with big brands offers an unspoken guarantee of quality.

Websites like SourceBottle always do shout-outs looking for professionals to offer their services for events. The most sought after are video and photography, lighting and sound, bands, singers, performers and MCs.

You probably need more money, not more work. I get it! But putting in your time to leverage new relationships is about growing. It comes down to what you want to get out of the deal. Think about doing it once every quarter. The exposure you receive may allow you to put up your fee.

The allure of the goodie bag and your name in every-one's hand

Everyone loves getting something for free, and you could get market research from it that would otherwise have cost you money. Getting a taste of your product might win them over to becoming customers.

At a fundraising event for a school, a local real estate agent donated her time to sell a house for free. The average commission on a $2 million house is about $40,000, so it was a great prize and the school benefited from the winning bid, which helped to build the new playground. The agency also got their name in the school newsletter for about three months, was invited to the cocktail party at the school to mingle with the parents and got to tell their story to lots of local families who lived in the community. That one prize went buzzing through the whole area and their name was everywhere. Even the local paper did an article on them being so charitable. It's possible they were hired to sell at least another ten houses in the local area and parents remembered it for years afterwards.

You do not have to give away thousands of dollars. Start with a voucher. You could offer $20 off a customer's first purchase or 20% off a meal at your restaurant. If you have a product, you could provide a sample of your new hand cream for free – as long as they register with their email address, of course!

Get your product used at an event – real-time sampling

You could also do a deal with the organisers of an event to contribute and get naming rights. This works well with food and beverage providers or products used on the dining tables at an event. I've seen impressive grazing tables created with signage to promote the supplier too.

Glasshouse candles are known to be the highest quality in the market and are a lovely gift to say 'thank you for coming'. People know the value of each candle is $50 each. You could negotiate with a supplier to buy a gift at cost or wholesale to have a mention at the event. Or you could offer some seats at the event for their staff as a trade, so you can do some networking.

If this is leaving you sweating at the cost and volume, think small. You could offer a lucky door prize with one of your products.

Later in the book, we will go through how to negotiate these points. There are some assets that do not have a cost, but products have a real and definite cost and you need to ensure a good return on your investment.

SNAPSHOT

Partnerships are varied and diverse, so you must know what outcome you want before you start to approach companies. Begin with the partners you unofficially have a referral system with already then work outwards from there.

Keep it simple. Understand what you are trying to achieve but approach the partnership model with the customer in mind. What could you create that your customers would love and has great value for them? When you approach a partner, show them you have the customer in mind as your priority. The way to get action is to illustrate how they can benefit before you ask for what you want.

In the next chapter, we'll look at the value you are sitting on in your business that other companies would love to have. It's important to understand the value you can offer to your partner and know how to talk about the opportunities.

Chapter 3
LET'S TALK ABOUT YOU

KNOW YOUR VALUE

You've dreamt about creating your own business and now you have it! This is a huge achievement, and many people never bring their dream to life. You should be so proud. I also know that even though it's 100 times sweeter that you thought it would be, it's 1,000 times harder too.

The hardest part is wearing all the hats! Many people have a sweet spot or a craft they are great at – maybe cake decorating, numbers or making people sweat as a personal trainer. The reality is you must also look after sales, marketing, logistics, production, finance, legal contracts, hiring staff and a host of other functions you've probably had no experience with.

You've learnt many skills and procedures along your journey, and this knowledge, along with the relationships you've built, are now an asset you have in your business. If you decided to sell your business tomorrow, could someone jump straight into it? When it's running perfectly, it's testament that you have built a viable trading company.

Your company is different to your brand though. A brand is the way a product or service is perceived by those who experience it. It's more than a logo or a name; a brand is the recognisable feeling these assets evoke. The reason your customers come back to your brand is a collection of elements they experience. Some are constructed by your company on purpose, while others are delivered by the service your staff offer or how the product performs in their hands.

It's important you understand how your brand appears and the way you engineer and present it to your potential partners. You want to make it evident you are a professional and both companies can be transparent about how they can work together.

Many small companies don't realise the value they are sitting on, so they play it small. I appreciate that marketing may not be your craft or in your skill set, and you might be more suited to the numbers or the manufacturing, but you know as well as I do, there are no sales without some selling. However, when you are passionate about the company, sharing how you can help others is the simplest form of selling.

It's incredibly valuable for you to be able to:

- Clearly articulate your business so people can remember it.
- Know your customers and what they expect from your brand.
- Know all the assets in your business that are valuable.
- Present your business in a concise, confident way.

THE ULTIMATE ONE-LINER

How to have a business people remember
Tell me what you want to be known for?

It is important to understand what you do and be able to present it in a way that's interesting, memorable and separates you from your competitors. Every time you meet someone new, there's an opportunity for you to promote your business and create a promoter, customer or fan. However, most people struggle to have the confidence to do this.

Americans are great at promoting themselves and we should learn from them. Australians are a lot more laid back and don't want to be the tall poppy in the room. By having a great one-liner, you are inviting others to have a conversation.

Whether it's a social, school function or a business meeting, people always ask what you do for a living. Simply saying IT makes it quite a closed conversation. It feels like a shut down. The other person might politely say, 'Who do you work for?' or, 'What area of IT?' but that will probably be it as they have nothing left and don't want to pry since you appear to not want to talk about it.

Having a simple dose of confidence invites others into the conversation.

If people can remember what you do then they will share your story. In the book *Key Person of Influence* by Daniel Priestley, he outlines a really simple way of doing this.

- **Name** – saying your first name and surname plus the company name slowly and clearly is an important first step. How many times have people stood in front of you and said their name so quickly you don't remember it a second later?
- **Same** – people have crazy titles that no-one understands. Is that IT or HR?? Choose a title that others know and recognise such as marketing, HR, interior designer, engineer, teacher.
- **Claim to fame** – what do you do that sums up who you serve and the result they get from working with you?

    The best examples I heard, and consequently have remembered, were two people I met that were able to articulate what they did succinctly, while inviting a conversation to commence.

1. I am Andrew from the Cyber Resilience Institute. I'm a

cyber security expert and I keep the top 100 CEOs out of the courtroom and in the boardroom.

2. I am Jen Dugard and I'm a personal trainer. I help mums get a better body after babies.

If you have longer, you can tell them how you do it.

I have a six-week plan that allows sleep-deprived mums to follow a healthy eating plan to maximise their energy and tie that into an exercise program that involves their baby so they can do it at home or in our group classes and are left feeling strong and supported by other mums.

Immediately I want to know more, right? Where are the classes? How long have you been doing this? Can you keep going until the baby is older? Is it a diet or can I have some treats occasionally?

Two things happen:

1. This allows the other person to engage in a conversation and ask questions. You get to talk more about your business without feeling like you're self-promoting.

2. It's memorable and allows them to tell others simply. Often what happens is people say, 'I know someone who needs that,' or, 'I know someone you should talk to.' It could even be, 'Have you thought of partnering with a food delivery service? I know someone I could put you in contact with.'

Don't think small: 'Well I'm just a small business that offers pottery classes.' No, you help mums escape to a tranquil space to create a handmade piece of pottery with love, while enjoying a drink and a laugh with a group of like-minded women.

Engineer an introduction

Knowing what you would like to grow into is another step. It's okay to then ask others to assist you at the end of these conversations. Most people like to help if they know what you need help with.

When I had my business, I bought Jeep strollers from the USA licensee and that worked well, but culturally, there were other products I needed for the Australian marketplace. At that stage I did not know what it took to be a licensee myself.

I reached out to someone who owned a licensing agency in Australia. I told them what I'd been able to achieve with my business and the retailers I was working with. I then explained that Australia had cultural requirements different from the USA and asked advice on how to become a licensee myself.

I knew where I wanted to go but didn't know how to get there. Reaching out to this agency was amazing as they taught me what I needed to do. The benefit to them was they now knew someone to recommend to their other licensors who could bring their products to Australia, as I already had the retailer supply chain sorted. We were able to help each other.

Think about your next step

- What does success look like in your mind?
- What is your vision to bring the business to that point?
- Who knows the answer to your questions on how to get there?
- Who already has a solution you could work with?
- Who else would benefit if you're successful?

Like me, you may have a group of independent retailers and want to get into the big retail chains. Find someone who is already there and ask them how they did it and what challenges they had. There's plenty to learn as many retailers have requirements around standards testing, integration into an ordering system, warranty procedures or they may want to ensure you have copyright for the region.

Perhaps you are happy with your current business position, but want to increase your billing to your current customers. In the same way, you can ask others how they grew. It's also okay to ask your customers what else they need and what other services they are buying, and you may be able to service that need for them.

Realising what you need takes courage to look at your business objectively. It could be you actually need funding or a third-party warehouse service who can pick and send your orders, as your house is overrun with stock and you can't move down your hallway anymore. It's about understanding what you need to move past this current point in your business.

MAP YOUR BRAND ON A PAGE

Now you have a better idea of where you want to go, it's time to map it out on a piece of paper so you can stick it on your wall. Having this clarity allows you to make good business decisions. If a choice or business decision does not align with one of these elements, then it's an easy NO.

It is time to create a brand on page. Clearly, some businesses need a full marketing strategy and I'd definitely encourage you to explore this in detail, but if you create a twenty-page document and it sits in your drawer all year, then there is no value. Brand marketing is an approach to communications, sales product and service that grow the assets of brand equity. It's the process where a business makes itself known to the public and differentiates from its competitors. A brand on a page keeps you clear on how to pitch your business, focused on what you want to achieve and the values that are important to you.

Even multi-million-dollar companies use a brand on a page. I consulted to a global company who was the leader in their category and a sought-after brand in the industry. Its value is not only important to the leader of the business but also the staff. Other departments like supply chains, warehousing and product development all benefit from having a simple clear view of the business to help them access new decisions.

Brand on a Page				
Brand Vision	Apple wants everyone in the world to be part of it's future			
Purpose	At Apple, we want to make a dent in the universe by challenging the status quo and thinking differently. We believe equally in art and technology.			
Values	Consumer first, simplicity and ease-of-us, stylish designs, fast to market, community.			
The Big Idea: Apple makes technology so simple that everyone can be part of the future.				
Promise: We make it so easy to use electronics, that you will feel smarter and at the leading edge of technology.	Strategy: Technology with stylish designs made simple & consumer friendly stretching across a broad range of electronic products.	Story: Technology shouldn't be intimidating or frustrating. We make it simple enough so you can be engaged right away.	Freshness: Surprising technology that changes the world. Every product is stylish, simple, easy to use & leap frogged competitors.	Experience: Apple starts with the consumer experience & works back to the technology, eliminating frustrations
Goals	Continue 10% sales growth, double market share in Asia, launch 5 new technologies per year.			
Strategies	Regain lead in smart phone technology	Geographic focus into China	Build around Cloud Technology	High Service to tighten Apple community
Tactics	Size options	Specific products	Launch into TV's	Take services online
	Win on design	Brand building	Integrate retail purchasing	Increase courses
	Launch watch	Launch watch		New retail spaces

Source: Graham Robertson - Linkedin

- Brand vision – why does your company exist?
- Your purpose – the reasons to believe you can do this and your *why*.
- The values – the emotional benefits or how you would speak about why you created your product/service.
- The big idea – this includes the promise to the customer, the strategy you adopt, your *why* story, your freshness or what is unique compared to others and how you want your customer experience to be.
- Goals for the company that are specific, measurable, actionable, realistic and time bound.
- The strategies for how you will achieve your goal.
- The tactics on how you will achieve the strategies.

If you are thinking, *I am a craftsman/interior designer/ accountant. I'm reading this book for you to tell me the answers and this is way too hard*, my advice is to let is just come out of you. Don't try to have dazzling answers. This document is for you and your business. Write it in an authentic way that encapsulates your voice, tone and feeling. Or ask your staff the questions and grab a whiteboard to find the common responses. It's really hard to get down to one sentence for each, especially if you have a whiteboard with a hundred responses, however, this is just your best thinking about how you want to approach the next few years in business.

KNOW YOUR CUSTOMERS INTIMATELY

To create a successful business, you need to know your customers well.

Think of your favourite customer.

- Where do they live?
- What do they do for work?

- Do they have kids? How old are they? Are they babies? Are they teenagers?
- What are their hobbies? Are they really into food?
- What are their spend limits?
- Are they more Mazda or BMW?
- What do they do for fun and where do they go?

Deep dive on your customer and create a persona, with a picture and a name. Then have that on your wall. When you're looking for information and you're looking for what partnerships you should be doing, look at that persona of your customer and ask, *Where would they look for this information? What would they do? Where would they go? Who would they shop with?* This will give you a clear idea of what you need to do.

If you don't have a clear idea of the customer, then it's hard to imagine who else is serving the same customer. You need to think wider and deeper. We are all multi-dimensional. If your target customer is a gin drinker, do not just think of the bars she would go to or what food she would eat while she is having a gin, but think about where she would go away on a long weekend, who she would travel with and how she'd book that holiday. These are all potential partners. The hardest part will be opening your mind to come up with possibilities. We can all come up with the first three companies, but the next ten are a little bit harder.

A product-focused business is one where you create a product, and then customers decide if they want it or not. A customer-focused business is about creating a product that solves a problem and communicating that pain point and solution so customers can gain. I assume you have a great product that your customers love because it solves a problem for them. I'm also going to trust you have a group of customers already that could be fifty or 5,000.

You need to be able to paint a picture of your customer so

you can engage with them, but also so you can find other companies who share the same type of customer. They allow your team to know about your customers or users at a deeper level, which improves your conversion rate.

Building a customer persona will ensure your marketing efforts yield maximum returns for your business. When you develop an understanding of the desires and behaviours of your customer, you can make decisions strategically instead of intuitively. When I know the customer well, the marketing feels like it was made just for them. It is targeted and speaks to the customer, instead of being broad and generalised.

Think of a customer persona as a cheat sheet; a quick one-pager you have to sense-check your marketing, customer service and sales decisions. The best part is this persona development process will give you the meaningful data about your target audience you've been craving.

If you are starting out and only have a few customers, it's still worth doing the exercise so you can service those customers in such a way that they will buy more from you and recommend you to friends or business contacts.

The information you are seeking about your customer can be obtained in multiple ways, but essentially you are either going to use data that is available from their digital footprint or you are going to ask them outright. There is quantitative data where you get numbers and percentages, and qualitative data where you get insights from their answers.

Do a data dive to get a realistic persona

Using digital platforms and your accounting software, you can look at their orders to gain their location, sex, business type, order frequency, product selection. You can use social media to look at the comments and questions they ask, plus questions via your website. Google analytics, Facebook and Instagram dashboards will also help you. Here's a good start:

- Demographic data – age, gender, estimated income bracket, geography, family size.
- Psychographic – goals, challenges, personality type, motivations.
- Professional details (especially if you're in the B2B market) – job title and role level, decision-making power, industry.
- Personal tastes and interests – publications or magazines they read, blogs, articles or forums they read.
- *Bonus info – a photo that reflects your target user/customers plus a fictional paragraph that tells their story with a few quotes that reflect their desires.

Qualitative data is where people answer questions directly and this is the most valuable as it is straight from their mouth. The skill here is to ask the right questions and extract the information while not asking leading questions that get you the information you want them to say. The mistake many people make is making assumptions about their customer, based on what they think is the case, or sometimes how they feel about the product. If you are going to ask your customers directly, then tools like SurveyMonkey let you gather information quickly.

When you are doing qualitative research and asking questions, these are more specific:

- What problem does our product solve for you or what do you want to achieve by using our product?
- What's your biggest pain point? What frustrates you? How often do you encounter this problem?
- How has our [product feature] impacted your work? How do you measure success in your role?

When I was in the baby industry, I distributed a product from Brazil called Baby Cubes that allowed mums to create and store small amounts of baby food for when their kids were starting solids. It sold so well in the nursery and baby goods areas of stores, especially in Big W. After asking parents for their feedback, I found out the parents themselves used the small containers to take to work with salad dressing and portion control items like nuts and cheese for their lunch.

This information allowed me to target a large homewares chain, rebadge the product and create a new distribution channel for the product. I would never have had the new channel for sales had I not asked my customers some questions.

There are so many specialist websites which concentrate on creating customer persona templates, so I encourage you to explore these in detail. I am just giving you an overview of where to start.

If you are feeling like it is an intrusion to your customers to ask them questions, then incentivise them. Most customers are open to doing a short survey. It's amazing what the allure of a gift voucher or a percentage off their next order will motivate people to do. It will differ slightly if you are business-to-business (B2B) or business-to-customer (B2C), ecommerce or you sell only through distributors and not directly to your customer. The aim is just to get the best image you can.

Relevance will make it easier to see your customer and speak in their language. The biggest mistake you can make is to touch the surface and be general e.g. women thirty to fifty who live in a metro city with two kids. The thirty year old woman who is juggling two kids under five and part-time work, looks very different to a mother in her late forties with kids finishing high school having driving lessons. If you try to speak to them in the same way, you won't resonate with either of them.

Partners are looking for an edge too

Your perfect partner will have a similar target market and be from a complimentary industry. Your goals will align. Having the same target customer is the most logical match. Think of this in terms of, *Would this customer put my product and their product in the same shopping cart?* Also think a little wider than that about industries that may be complementary – food and wine, for example.

YOU ARE ALREADY SITTING ON A TONNE OF VALUE THAT OTHER COMPANIES WANT

You may be surprised to find you have a huge amount of value in your business. These are your assets; the things you have built up in your business that you own. If you were to sell your company, they are all the things of value the new owner would want. When I talk about leverage, I use it as per general dictionary definitions, 'To use something you have, to create something new or better.' Another definition is, 'The power to influence results,' which is fitting too. You are sitting on a goldmine that other companies would love, so you can share assets to get ahead.

What do you have in your business that helps your brand and your company sell your products?

I bet you've never sat down and done a stocktake of the value you have available. Imagine you were approached by a competitor who wanted to buy your business, you'd have to assess the assets you've built and know the value those assets have to other people. If you cannot show your value, you will be undervalued. It's your time to puff out your chest and be proud of what you have built.

When I decided the time was right to sell my business, I approached one of my favourite customers and asked if he knew anyone within the industry who might be interested. He replied that *he* was! Once you know the value of your assets within your company, it's all about negotiating the best deal possible. It's not dissimilar to doing a partnership.

Now's the time to make yourself irresistible, as attractive as you can to the other partner, highlighting all your strengths and presenting your weaknesses as opportunities for growth. This task is about credibility and professionalism. You might only have five customers, but they are the CEOs of the five biggest insurance companies or car manufacturers. It's not just about numbers.

There are plenty of books about getting your business ready for sale and I can tell you from firsthand experience, books like *The 4-Hour Work Week* by Timothy Ferriss is a classic, and I still have a framework I would use today. But mostly, this is about setting up a system so anyone can come in and take over. If the business relies on you to function, it's not nearly as saleable as one that has procedures in place to make it easy for others to take over. If you are interested in selling, this is not your book. However, the assets you will build through partnerships will add value to your business when you do want to sell.

I can hear your shoulders slump – you're not sure about this. Not only will this task become one of the most valuable things you can do for your business, it will be something you can be proud of.

LET'S START WITH YOUR PRODUCT OR SERVICE

What is it you sell every day?

It's not just your products that are valuable, but also the manufacturing process and procedures, contacts and insights you have. The first point to explore is where your knowledge and physical product could be used to create a partnership. This is the product you are known for and has sales attached to it – it's transparent.

When I had my business, I had products I manufactured. I invested in tooling, safety compliance and testing, printing my own fabric, as well as artwork for the packaging. The costs were high, and that didn't even take into account the year it had taken a team of people to make the product come to life. It's hard to put that into the product cost.

Compare that to the lines of products I had available from my large partners overseas. I grew to a point where I could go into Toys "R" Us with an image of a product and sell them a whole container's worth of the product. I simply placed an order and arranged the shipping straight to them, sending them an invoice. I did not touch the product at all. I could make $10,000 profit on each product with one meeting and a few emails. Perfection! That relationship was worth a million bucks!

Start with a list of all your products or services and how they are created. Look at the process in detail:

- What is the manufacturing process for the products? Also know the cost of goods.
- Your relationship with the factories where you create the product and the standard or safety compliance you need to understand to be able to sell the product in Australia.
- Tooling, fabric creation or machines that you have invested in that are at your disposal that other brands can't get to.
- Distinctiveness of the product in the marketplace.
- What other products could you or your manufacturer make?
- Could you change the recipe and create a co-branded product?

Like my example above, what else is available for you to sell? I'm not going to go down to balance sheet level here, but what I am showing you is what you can leverage.

These are your babies. The things you have created. Products are easier to qualify, but if you were an interior designer this could be your process and procedures, your wholesale relationship access to get things first and the style you are known for.

Place of purchase or distribution

You clearly sell products, so what channels do you have to get the products to market? These could be your physical location if you are a restaurant or a store, your website if you are ecommerce or it could be retailers who stock your product. Others want what they do not have. Your sales channels are where your customers transact and are one of your most valuable assets.

One of my favourite brands, a decade ago, and a great example of virtual to physical, was Shoes of Prey – a bespoke shoe creator. You got to choose the shape, colour, heel size, strap, material etc. They built an amazing reputation to the point where David Jones invited them to have a concession area (like a pop-up) in three of their city locations. This gave David Jones extra foot traffic into their stores and increased sales in other areas. It gave Shoes of Prey the chance to have a physical location where people could try on the shoes, along with the brand association of such an established, well-regarded retailer for credibility. Mimco also started off this way before opening their own stores.

If you have a product, do you sell directly off your website? Are you listed on other websites? Are you stocked in any independent retailers and how many? Are you in any major chains?

If you have a service like a marketing agency, understand how you get your work. We met an agency at a conference and have spent about $500,000 with them. Do you come up on page one when I search marketing agencies in Brisbane on Google? And does your website have lots of content that is regularly downloaded and trusted as a credible source to the industry or are you invited to speak at events as you are acknowledged as the go-to agency in that space?

Have you got venue space or a retail location that has foot traffic or is an in-demand location for events? What about the signage for the car traffic that passes your location? You could have unique signage effectively negating the need for billboard advertising.

Owned channels to communicate

'Owned assets' is a marketing term that means if you want to put a message out to the market, where could you place it that you have control of? One of the biggest differences between dealing with influencers on Instagram and dealing with companies are the breadth of avenues for them to promote.

When I was at GraysOnline, an online auction company, their biggest asset was their traffic to their website, but also their data, since they sell everything from trucks to diamond rings and bottles of wine.

One marketing initiative I introduced was take the company to the HIA Home Show to meet customers who were interested in renovation products. I offered $20 off their first order and showed them the thousands of products that sold for less than $20 each week.

Most customer's first purchase is a case of wine. Like many ecommerce websites, if you secure the first transaction, you can serve them other enticing items. The cost of exhibiting at the expo was around $3,000 but resulted in thousands of new customers and in only one year, those customers had purchased more than $3 million worth of products.

Let's do a stocktake of everything you have at your disposal:

- Website – site traffic, search ranking, product rating or review, ecommerce.
- Social pages – engagement, followers, YouTube views, LinkedIn network.
- Networks/associations/memberships you are active in
- Database – customers, prospects, open rates.
- Content creation – what you do well like videos, blogs or write for publications.
- Research – what do you know that others would love to know?
- Press coverage – do media seek out your comments?

Don't be shy here. Remember, if you were selling your business, you'd be listing all these assets and putting a value on each and every one.

Person or figurehead of the business

Remember the biggest asset for your company could be your own personal brand and how it is regarded in your industry. Do a stocktake on yourself, or the figurehead of the business, as people don't buy products and services, they buy *you*. How many times have you heard a story where a company sets up an advisory board and attracts someone like the head of product development for Google or Jeff David, the founder of Petbarn? Your position also attracts attention. Go to a marketing conference and there may be someone from Amazon speaking, it could be the new hot player. Nick Molnar from Afterpay is sought after, as he has taken an idea to a billion-dollar company, and he's still in his thirties. How can your previous positions and credibility count in your assets?

Start with your history, as well as the credibility of your staff, advisors and partners.

- Previous positions can show credibility, such as, 'Was the head fashion buyer at David Jones and now has her own fashion brand.' Bring in company names and roles to show you have a good pedigree.
- Skill set – do you have a history of launching products or starting new communities?
- Awards or titles – were you a finalist in the Telstra businesswoman awards, B&T's top thirty under thirty, Dux at Sydney University, judge on a TV show?
- Have you been published by media as an authority in the industry? This elevates your status quickly as the perception is that you are a reliable and respected figure.
- Is your brand known in the industry for something

remarkable? Futureflip is known for building bespoke homes in sixteen weeks.

- Trustworthiness – can you demonstrate you made a profit in a recession, increased market share in a different country or were hired by a new CEO to make change?
- Is your name recognised, such as McGuigan – a winemaking family? Or Waterhouse – horse trainers? Or perhaps you have built a brand for yourself like Naomi Simson from RedBalloon.
- Are you on the board or panel for an industry association?
- Are you known for your ability to speak on stage like a Ted Talk?

Do not exclude others in your business. Include everyone you can to show your credibility. Use your LinkedIn profile and your staff as a starting point and grow from there. Talk about your team like you were recommending them for a job.

SNAPSHOT

You now have a comprehensive pitch of your business message, an understanding or snapshot of your customer persona and a stocktake list of the valuable assets you have within your company. You've completed the first step, and in my opinion, the most important one. Without being able to sell yourself, you cannot expect your potential partners to jump onboard.

Go to my website www.theresetarlinton.com where you can download a partnership checklist to help you with this process.

This is a task you should be doing every year or so. As your business grows or changes you need to update this to be clear on what you can leverage. It takes time and patience to work *on* your business instead of *in* your business. If you have others in your company, it would be wise to include them in this task, as the perspective of the logistics person would be different to the customer service person.

Now you have it all together, document it and start sharing to get a little feedback. You should have a functional, detailed one for your staff and advisors etc. and another punchy one or two-page snapshot version you can send to a potential partner. Make sure this reflects your brand by using your brand colours and fonts, plus imagery of your products or lifestyle shots.

Now you understand what the partnership options are, it's time to start looking at companies you would like to work with. Look for a partner who has the same values as you. It's important to make sure you are aligned and you have done your research on them. You want to ensure your first connection gets you the reaction you want: a first conversation.

Chapter 4
FINDING A COMPATIBLE PARTNER

You've probably dreamed about doing business with a certain brand and have an idealistic view of what they could do for your business, catapulting you into the level of success you covet. The reality is, most deals don't get the desired outcome because simple steps are not taken.

To understand what your business needs in a partner, research is the first step. Essentially, you are going to look behind the curtain to see if they tick the boxes *before* you make contact. I want you to be confident connecting with the right partners and be able to do so easily. Don't try to convert them in the first email, you need to have a pitch to get to a first conversation. This allows you to have a scoping conversation about the possibilities, and gives you the chance to demonstrate your suitability as a partner.

BIG BRANDS NEED WHAT SMALL BRANDS HAVE

You can offer a partnership that will deliver assets they couldn't create themselves. However, like any relationship, there are necessary ingredients to make it work. Understand the science behind the deal so you can assess its worth and the art of trusting your gut to ensure your partnership feels good. If you do not assess the partnership potential and how you could work together for the benefit of the customer, then you may as well just have dinner together and be friends.

A partnership takes effort; an investment of your time and energy. It requires a commitment to create a promotion around a common theme. When it's good, it can take you to a position you might never have been able to reach yourself. Occasionally though, deals do turn sour and rob you of your time through actions that were not addressed. What we are discovering in this chapter are the tools to judge a partner, reach out and connect, then determine if it's a good match.

In my twenty years of partnerships, I still learn from each one. Every learning makes the next deal better, more secure, more generous and more valuable. I want to share my experiences so you won't be one of *those* brands that goes in wide-eyed and excited, and ends up disappointed.

I've done deals with brands brokered through talent and public relations agencies who have a remit to justify their retainer and royalty payment. Many staff in agencies are young and hungry for the next role and move onto the next agency way before the deal is over, leaving the possibility that – through no fault of yours or your partner's – neither of you actually get what you need. Of course, the next staff member tries to go through the emails, but since there were so many conversations, there isn't any evidence of commitment or ideas on what was supposed to happen.

Remember, partnerships are about two companies doing a deal to benefit their mutual customers, while both growing and gaining in the process. They are done in a spirit and fashion that allows for generosity and ambiguity.

In this chapter, we are going to cover:

• How to look for the partnership potential.

- Reaching out and scoring your first conversation.
- Seeing if you are compatible and knowing how to exit if you're not.

YOUR SIMPLE FIRST STEP

Each partner must have a goal

Each party must have a goal but they do not have to be the same goal. An established brand's goal could be to engage with a younger, more social audience, whereas a new brand could be about borrowing the credibility of the established brand to build trust so the consumer will transact.

For example, the luxury brand Louis Vuitton, very well established, did a capsule range with a very new hip rapper from New York. As a result, Louis Vuitton increased their sales by 30% in that quarter because they attracted a new customer and demographic who had not purchased from them before. The rapper was able to create not only a profitable clothing range for his brand, but his relationship with Louis Vuitton enabled him to create a range with another retailer.

There are many possibilities of who you can partner with and my proven methodology will help you find the right partners. Be clear on what you want to achieve. Don't think that one partnership is going to get you everything you want. It's better to have achieved one goal and have a happy customer and happy partner rather than trying to accomplish ten things, while the partnership turns out to be weak and the customer is not happy.

Your goals can overlap. If your metric is about click-throughs to your website so you can capture an email address, then obviously if you got incremental sales as a by-product of that, you would be happy. You can achieve multiple goals, but it's important to set out with one clear ambition.

BEING A FAN OF A BRAND DOESN'T MEAN YOU ARE A PARTNERSHIP MATCH

The partner you are looking for is the brand that will give you what you need, at the right time in your business. When you started reading this book, I bet you had a partner in mind. Let's look more closely to see if they are a good fit and why you have an attraction to them, as Mr Right may be Mr Not Right Now.

A partnership with a big fish is completely possible. When I started my company I did a deal with Huggies nappies. They approached me through their promotions agency and asked me to contribute six Jeep baby strollers for a competition they were going to run (which was less than $1,000 cost of goods for the products). It felt like a great opportunity, so I went for it without question. If I'd had some experience in partnerships, I would have asked for more and contributed more. I was quite a passive partner at the time.

The deal skyrocketed my company, as the stroller was on the point-of-sale advertising in every Coles supermarket nationally. It was the type of exposure I couldn't afford for my business. I jumped in as I knew the Huggies brand was a leader in their category and had the same target customer as my brand: new mothers.

So, if you are the company who wants to approach another brand, then it's time to do some research to ensure you are aligned and the compatibility is obvious.

DO A STOCKTAKE OF THE BRAND YOU'D LIKE TO WORK WITH

- What are they known for? Are they the leader in their category or industry?
- What product or service do they offer?

- Who are their customers? Would these people buy your product?
- Is it national, local or international? How far do you want the partnership to go?
- Who are their stockists? Could this open doors for you into retail channels?
- Do they own their own retail outlets? How many and where are they located?
- Who owns the company? If it is privately owned, then it may be easier to deal with them versus if they are a listed company with shareholders.
- Who is the figurehead or leader of the company? What do they stand for? Who can relate to them?

Now that you've looked at the company in detail, are there any characteristics that draw you closer or make you take a step back? You wouldn't hire an agency or take on a new customer without doing a bit of research and this is no different. If anything, it will give you points to discuss at the next step.

What does their digital footprint tell you?

Examine the information freely available to understand where your potential partners sit in the market and what their customers love or hate about them. Their digital footprint will provide insights that can give you an advantage.

If you were considering a local hairdresser, then you learned a friend had already been there, wouldn't you get their opinion before you decided to go? One person's opinion might not be enough to make a decision but getting comments from many people will give you a direction to lean into. I wouldn't book a holiday without looking at Tripadvisor or buy a new oven without checking productreview.com.au.

Take a look at reviews from customers

- Search the brand online and see if there are reviews. Where do they appear? SEO should have them on the first page.
- Look for positive and negative reviews. Look in depth at five of their posts that have the most comments to understand the sentiment of the brand on consumer channels like Instagram and Facebook.
- Read the comments on five LinkedIn posts to gauge the sentiment of the founder or person running the company, or a marketing lead you want to connect with.
- Watch any interviews on YouTube by the management and reviews of the products done by others. Look at the comments on these videos.

If you think you're not a digital native and can't find what you need, Google, YouTube and Facebook and twenty minutes after dinner will give you a good feel.

What ideas are springing to mind on how you could partner with your desired brand? Remember, small companies have what big companies need. Big companies have power and pull, but they are heavy and slow to turn. Small is nimble, fresh, focused and driven – all characteristics that are irresistible to big businesses.

Research will reveal areas where you are compatible and what you can offer them

When it's time to reach out, remember that brands know the people who have made the effort to do twenty minutes of research and tailor their pitch to the company. I recently had a company approach me and they didn't even know what products we manufactured. I usually give them the benefit of the doubt and reply asking how they think we could work together. If the reply is all about what I can do for them, a quick 'No, thanks' follows.

I have been a small company dealing with big brands. Now I work with the big brands, seeking out small businesses to work with. However, when I deal with the Nine Network and *The Block*, I become the small company to them. Remember there is always a bigger fish.

THE SECRET SAUCE IS TO ALWAYS DEMONSTRATE MUTUALITY

The customer should ultimately be the winner when two brands work together. This is alluring, especially for big companies and brands that can sometimes lack personality. Put yourself in your mutual customers' shoes.

- What would help them? What would they like to see?
- What customer groups do you have that would love to hear about their product?
- How could your brand demonstrate the partner's product to your audience?
- What FAQs could you answer by integrating the partner's product or service?
- Where are they lacking that you could create content? Videos, articles, podcasts or co-developing a product?
- What could you pitch that would whet their appetite to have a conversation?

If you think your ideas might not be on point and are going to put them off, please don't worry. If you are showing them how you can help but haven't quite hit the mark, they'll appreciate the effort. About 99% of brands who approach big companies to ask about partnerships never even make a tiny effort, they only talk about themselves.

Just think about how you would feel if you got an enthusiastic approach where a brand had taken the time to research how your customer could benefit from a collaboration. Wouldn't you be chuffed? They chose your company before thousands of others because they recognised the potential. That's what you are doing for other brands.

CONNECTING WITH A PARTNER TAKES COURAGE, BUT THEY'RE JUST LIKE YOU

Using your mutual customer as the reason for connecting is immediately going to separate you from the hundreds of others who send a blanket email. Finding the right person to reach out to at a company isn't simple, but it's not hard either. Searching online has made it easier to connect than ever before and connecting with the right person is your best shot for success. You're solving a problem they have.

I really wanted to work with CSR as they are the best in the business, but I was afraid my entrepreneurial journey didn't match their corporate criteria. The role closed before I could apply, and at that point, I decided I really wanted to be part of their company. I called reception and addressed the person by name – Jacqui. I said I wanted to speak to Sam in recruitment as I thought he was the right person I'd looked at on Linkedin, and I explained that the job had been taken down. I gave my best shot at connecting with Jacqui and asked for her help. She not only got my CV to the right person but wrote a great message saying how lovely I was to her on the phone. If it weren't for her, I wouldn't have landed the role, as my application wouldn't have gone to the right person in time. Most people are gracious. Connect with them personally and they will reply.

Now you've got the contact, you need to make the first move. You're not looking for commitment, just a first conversation. What can you include in the conversation that will make them want more? Too much information makes it easy for them to decide without you.

From your research, you should have a few people within the company you've seen on YouTube or who have been interviewed in the press. You could connect with them on LinkedIn or ask a mutual contact to connect you. A warm introduction is always going to be your best option. This could also be through an agency they work with or a partner they've worked with before – anyone who is willing to introduce you. This is the traditional way, of course, so you know how to do this.

The social way is to send a DM on their social media channels asking for the right person to contact about a partnership. This works better than calling the company reception, as the person answering the DMs is more likely to be in the marketing department. When social posts are being done through an agency, they will pass it on for fear of retribution.

Once you find the right person, get their email and mobile. If I have sent a message through reception, I usually try to connect on LinkedIn and say I'm waiting for their reply – anything to get them intrigued and prompt an action.

The most impressive message to initiate a response is a video message

Grab your phone and record a brief pitch. This style of message shows your personality and your enthusiasm, creates an emotional connection and demonstrates you are actively seeking a conversation. Remember, your research puts you in a strong position to demonstrate how you could work together.

What is the worst thing that could happen? If they aren't interested, you're no worse off than you were yesterday, but you might learn something that will allow you to connect with someone else in the industry.

An alluring, interesting and a compelling pitch will always get the attention it deserves

I recently received a pitch, via reception, from a project that had appeared in *Home Beautiful* in 1958 and is still recognised as one of the most architecturally significant homes in Sydney. The daughter of the original owner contacted us and shared a little about the house, attaching the article from 1958 with images of the home. The email asked me if I wanted to be part of bringing this home to life. Gyprock had been a part of its original story and could be again. I couldn't pick up the phone quick enough to say yes. She gave me enough information to assess for myself but left out the details so if I wanted more, I had to make the call. Very clever!

Just like a great media release, you want to address the five Ws and then HOW:

1. Who: Who you are? Remember your pitch? Name, same and claim to fame. Who else are you working with on the project that could be a complimentary stakeholder?
2. What: What are you doing of great interest to your mutual customer? What would you like to do with them?
3. When: This can vary. If you have a project with a timeline, you can add it here. You could also talk about timing as you've just come off a brilliant campaign to your mutual audience and they are hungry for more. You want to create a sense of urgency making it enticing to get in touch.
4. Where: This could be where you are doing this or where you could collaborate, e.g. on a product for a retailer like Target, on a digital product that you are constantly getting enquiries after or at an event for the 100 top CEOs where you will be the guest speaker.
5. Why: Why is this such a great idea and why should they contact you to discuss it? For example, *I thought it would be a great chance for you to share your company/product with our group of customers.*
6. How: How do they get in contact with you? How can they decide about you quickly? For example, your LinkedIn

profile, company website or invite them into your store/restaurant.

Make sure you include your double-page bio of what you've done to show credibility or a single page about a project – both with lots of images. Don't send the thirty-page PDF, just the top points to create interest. You can do this. Write this out and use it as a script for a conversation or an email. Unfortunately, if nothing changes, then nothing changes. Your partner needs a unique difference as much as you do. You are doing them a favour.

Always offer more than you ask for

Generosity is infectious. Offering more will show you are willing to give the customer something of value. We all have a friend who talks about themselves for an hour, and then, only when they have run out of steam, asks you how you are. When it's all one-sided, you switch off and it becomes boring.

Gyprock did a building collaboration with Soul Home, which has the holiday destination I mentioned in chapter two. However, during the construction, the builder with Soul Home recorded segments which weren't part of the agreement but showed me that they were willing to give a little more. These segments were created because when the builder was educating Simone from Soul Home, and as she was learning something new, she thought her audience would appreciate the information and be educated too. This became a reciprocal asset that Gyprock could benefit from too and was shared with their audience. Operating from that position made me want to work with Soul Home more and I also gave a lot more coverage than I had agreed to. Make it a love fest!

The aim is always for the customer to be the winner and gain. When you outline all the ways you can enhance the customer experience, this shows a strong position. Offer five things in the deal and ask for four things in return. I am not talking about giving away the farm, I'm suggesting small incremental values – including a note with your deliveries, an extra few tags on posts on Instagram, writing a bonus 200-word blog. It's another reason to elevate your partnership but shows your willingness for the deal to succeed. And let's be serious, your brand working with a big business name is only going to enhance your business standing. Partnerships are a dance. You're moving together in an elegant and entertaining way. This is not a solo ballet display.

COMPATIBILITY IS A MIX OF ART AND SCIENCE

Your partner might look good on paper, but compatibility is the secret ingredient to making something delicious. I'm going to assume you had your first conversation and it was good. You laughed, got to know each other and brainstormed a few ideas. You left each other feeling like this was an opportunity. Now what?

Operating with the same measure of success will keep your decisions pure. If you have a large brand who can't make the time or is unwilling to contribute assets to the deal, then trust your gut. They might not be the right partner. Has your partner outlined in writing what they would be willing to give for the partnership to move forward? Some corporations have so many layers of bureaucracy it's hard to get a decision. There may also be logistical or procedural reasons why certain elements of a deal can't be done. For example, adding your product as a gift with a purchase can't occur if they aren't licensed to carry food on their trucks or their warehouse has robotic picking and your item is too fragile. Always assess whether they *can't* or *won't*. Can't allows you to explore possibilities, whereas won't is a shut door in your face.

Use your gut feelings to see if you are both operating with

the customer in mind or whether you are just bartering deliverables. You've done deals with suppliers, customers and vendors, you know the drill, assess how much you're willing to give.

The science of a successful deal

To make it worthwhile and justify the time, labour, energy and mind space, the customer must be the ultimate winner. However, if it's not going to meet your objectives, then take a deep breath and walk away.

When I do partnerships with people of influence in building houses, one of the deliverables is that I receive finished photography of the home once the furniture is in and the kids are happily sitting on the lounge. If they are increasing in profile or don't want to release images of their finished home, then that's a 'no deal' for me. I can get lots of images of display homes with our products. The reason I seek out partnership with other brands is the alignment in quality builds using our products and choosing our brand. It's also about an emotional connection to a product. The photos of a family who others recognise delivers this.

When you create your deal memo together, which we will cover in the next chapter, ensure you list what you are going to deliver to each other, including the amount, the date and all the important elements. For example, 'I want photos in a finished home with a cute child or dog in the image that makes a connection. I don't want an empty room.'

It's your decision to make on your legal position, but it doesn't matter what's written on the deal if you aren't prepared to pay legal representation to get it if necessary. If you are fighting for what you are entitled to with your partners, then the quality of the images, articles or product they agreed to deliver is going to be terrible. Most times, a conversation where an alternative is offered will get you over the line. This is basically a handshake deal. Stuff happens, but how you deal with it is the memory that will be made. Act like an idiot or hide from your responsibilities and you probably won't be addressed legally but you will be addressed professionally. Marketing people all help each other to find great partners and we ask for recommendations. If you're hard to work with, or don't deliver, that will get around.

Contract

If you're thinking, 'I would never do that, because I am honest and trustworthy,' remember there are outside forces that might come to light – like the recent COVID-19 pandemic and stock stuck overseas. Your third-party warehouse could go into liquidation or you could get divorced and your spouse seizes your bank account. Talk it out with your partner and come up with an alternative. Chances are, none of this will happen, but having an idea around what you could do if things go wrong will give you some confidence to proceed. I'm sure this won't be the end of your business, or theirs.

The art of working relationships

You want to work with people who have the same values. I once admired a woman in business for a decade and she became my business hero. I went to every event where she spoke and constantly commented on every post. An opportunity came up to partner with her and I felt all my dreams had come true. Once we started working together, I got to see how she treated her employees, and I didn't agree with her behaviour at all. She was lovely to customers but not to her young staff. By then the partnership had started so I ensured I delivered what I said I would, but the second I could move on, I did. It was a big learning for me. The values I hold true are non-negotiable. Sadly, not everyone in business is a match – even your heroes.

Ask your partner about other partnerships they've been involved with, what brands did that they loved and anything they did that annoyed them. If your radar goes off, trust it. It's important to trust your intuition. These partnership deals are done in good faith, and I have developed long-standing friendships with many partners over the years because we worked well together and developed a healthy respect for each other's skills and effort.

However, if you feel they don't have the same ethics, values or even passions for the deal that you have, then it's okay to acknowledge it and call it out. You haven't wasted your time. You have a learning you can take with you into other areas of your business and that's worth a lot more than money. If you don't get the gut feeling until after the deal is done, that's okay too. Serve your obligations, acknowledge where it didn't work and say your goodbyes.

However, this type of partnership is rare. Most collaborations are a meeting of enthusiastic and motivated people coming together. While you are putting the deal together, the universe will help you to find the right people at the right time and elevate your business. There is a saying: 'The harder I work, the luckier I get.' If you do the research and put in the effort to make the relationship work, there is a high chance it will work and deliver beyond your expectations.

If it doesn't work, don't take it as a sign that you shouldn't be doing deals. Remember, partnerships are ultimately about both companies growing and without money changing hands. In your business journey, this is just one element to helping you build your empire.

SNAPSHOT

Just like finding a partner in love, it takes effort to learn, understand and find the ingredients to work together successfully. Partnerships are short stories you can maximise to your advantage. Doing your research is important, allowing you to assess who you want to work with and the value you can add. Once you've made contact, that research allows for a great conversation.

It takes commitment and time to do the research but it's a learning you can carry with you, which will open your mind and spark ideas on how you can work together to grow both businesses. Once you have a connection, understanding the art and the science involved gives you the permission and ability to decide if it's the right partner for you.

To save yourself from heartbreak, it's best to research a few potential partners and contact them. On the off-chance they all want to work with you, it's a great position to be in and allows you to uncover the potential to space the deals over the year, in order for you to maximise each partnership.

Now you've decided who you want to work with and determined they are a good fit, it's time to do the deal.

In the next chapter we will look at negotiating a deal so you are both winners. This will provide clarity on what you are agreeing to, how it is structured for clarity and commitment, and illustrate your exposure and risk. The deal must be clear with times, dates and activities, so that if it had to be executed by someone else in your company or theirs, it would be evident what must happen by who and when. This is important as staff leave, conversations get forgotten and some deals take years to deliver. It's your greatest weapon to secure success for both parties.

Chapter 5
DO THE DEAL!

'Like the energy of a wave approaching the shore, collaborations build a momentum towards a common goal, the strength of which is only possible when people unite with a positive, shared intention.' – **Danielle James, Author of** ***Collaboration is where IT's at.***

So, you've found your ideal partner and been discussing the possibilities of how you could work together for the benefit of the customer. Now it's time to put a deal together so the rules are clear for both parties to be successful, but also to ensure you both receive the commitment and what was agreed.

It's important to have a deal memo or agreement in writing for many reasons. It provides a solid discussion that is agreed to, but also a document for complete clarity. In the absence of fact, there is ambiguity. You agreed that you'd get photos from your partner, but down the track you get low-res images that can only be used for three months. WHAT! Are you joking! That's not what we agreed. Actually, you did if you signed it off and didn't clarify it.

There's a risk, if you don't document concisely, that parties can under-deliver, or simply not deliver at all. If it's a handshake and a conversation, our memories can recall differently and elements that were agreed to may just be innocently forgotten. Staff changes will always have an impact and without an agreement, there's no obligation for a party to complete the deal.

As mentioned in chapter two, there are many different types of partnerships, most of which are done in good faith and don't involve lawyers and twenty-page contracts. If you're structuring a marketing partnership where there is significant cost involved to either party, or a product is being specifically produced for a third party, like a retailer, then I highly suggest you consult a lawyer for advice.

This chapter is going to give you a road map of what you should be negotiating with your partner and some of the elements that get glossed over that can come back to bite you. I will leave you to decide if you'd like to formalise the agreement legally.

In this chapter we are going to look at:

- How to agree on the value exchange – what elements are you going to give and what do you want them to give you back.
- Where to formalise an agreement and the elements you need to discuss like timeframes, image usage and back links.
- Who should you include in this agreement and storage of the very important images, articles, testimonials and videos?

In some partnerships, the completion and handover of a finished product can take years. As an example, there was a deal negotiated through an agency that represented a *The Block* contestant once they finished their series. They were renovating their first home and wanted product in exchange for creating marketing assets. Their bank took longer to approve than they thought, and they were doing the work on weekends while performing their full-time jobs. The person at the agency left and somehow, so did the paperwork. I came into the deal more than a year later when I got an email request for more product to be provided. Neither party could produce a deal memo and therefore a new deal had to be negotiated. However, the product had already been given so immediately that put the supplier at a disadvantage. The deal was resurrected but it was not a great experience for either party. Only good communication and a willingness for both parties to come to the table and agree got the deal through. The agency – well, they had got their commission a long time before – failed both parties. The moral is to always have an A4 page that you can produce with details of the agreement.

ITEMS TO EXCHANGE IN YOUR DEAL – THE ASSETS

This is where you become more powerful together than you are separately. Look at the strengths of each partner and offer to give them an asset to help them grow – and it's reciprocated. I think you should always offer more than you ask. It shows you are entering into the spirit of the transaction.

Remembering the biggest winner in this deal must be the customer, think about how you can deliver an element of surprise or delight into their lives. It could be a limited-edition product, a one-off event in an exclusive location or an interview video that will draw traffic.

You've agreed in principle, now you must work on the topline elements that will be seen by the customers where you are working together. This will help you navigate what elements you need to deliver to your partner.

By far, the greyest area is around valuing the assets you have in your business, and whether to put an actual dollar figure on them. You can go onto multiple influencer websites such as Wink Model, Tribe or The Influencer Agency and they will list the value of a single post based on your following. This is a great start and I think it's worth doing this activity so you know what the market rates are. Document them and put them aside. They may not be necessary but will give you a benchmark.

Like any professional, you get to decide your market position and what you charge for your experience. You can go on freelancer.com and look at hundreds of people who are charging by the hour and compare the costs. However, when you do this, you are only really comparing basic information and not how suitable they are to work with. The last thing you want is to become a commodity.

On sites like hipages.com.au, you can find and hire a tradesperson for your home upkeep or renovation by set scales of pay e.g. $70-100 per hour, but they also offer additional fields to differentiate, such as the star rating, customer testimonials, suburbs they work and the average size of the job. This allows you to make a more informed decision.

You want to know the dollar figures based on what an influencer will charge, but when you are entering into a partnership deal you are assessing the whole package – and your ability to give your mutual customer something they couldn't get before. **Partnerships are how businesses work together.**

Most partners come together because they already advocate for the brand and can see the possibilities. They are united in a common goal. Despite this, very few actually reach out and connect due to lack of confidence, thinking they won't be valued or because they don't have experience structuring a deal. In my opinion, the best way to value your assets is by finding out from your partner what they want to get from the deal, and then put a package together to meet their objective.

Creating packages is a great way to not become a commodity

1. Outline your platforms – from chapter three. This includes your product knowledge, digital communication channels and strengths, and your in-person experiences.

2. Your reach and engagement. These are numbers-based but you can give examples of your best posts so they can assess your communication style rather than just looking at a figure. Your engagement rate is the number of people who interact with your communications or content. If you post something and it only gets four likes, and no comments, then it's underperforming. An engaged audience will comment and share as they feel like the post is talking directly to them.

3. Industry and specialisation. Beauty, fashion and fitness are very lucky to have thousands of influencers who are skilled at creating good-looking content. If you're in wealth management, aged care or manufacture a specialised product only suitable for bricklayers, then this limits the number of potential partners. The good news is though, finding partners in these areas should be a little easier as they realise how difficult it is to find new ways to talk about their products or services without being sales-focused. You wouldn't hire a hairdresser to talk about a new type of tile grout, but they might be a great partner to talk about retirement housing options in a local area, since they have appointments with the residents every week.

4. The type of content that needs to be created and what they specialise in is important. Your ability to judge the time, energy and resources that go into producing the content will also show their suitability and what the reciprocal value exchange should be.

5. Usage rights have a very definite value. If you want to

collaborate on building a workshop, your right to take the attendees comments, images and video footage has a much higher value than if you just have a deal where you talk to the audience for five minutes and leave. Usage rights apply to the individual assets, where you can use them, the length of time you can use them for and if you are able to repurpose them into other assets. An image used for one post on Instagram has a very different value than a high-resolution image that can be used on a billboard, full page ad in a magazine or in a TV commercial.

6. Exclusivity has a value too. Would you like to see a partner working with your competitor the next week? It can relate to an industry, geographical region, product category, timeframe or role. I was an ambassador for LG Electronics for one year and it was documented in the contract that I couldn't appear in any videos or advertising for any other electronics manufacturer for that time period and another year afterwards. For complete clarity, this was a paid partnership and their right to exercise these restrictions was warranted.

Here's an example of a tiered offering:

Bronze sponsor	Silver sponsor	Gold sponsor
On the episodes:	On the episodes:	On the episodes:
Your logo on the closing credits	Your logo on the closing credits	Your logo on the closing credits
On social media:	On social media:	On social media:
1 x exclusive Instagram post	2 x exclusive Instagram posts	3 x exclusive Instagram posts
2 x Instagram stories	4 x Instagram stories	6 x Instagram stories
2 x Instagram tagged stories	3 x Instagram tagged stories	4 x Instagram tagged stories
2 x exclusive Facebook posts	3 x exclusive Facebook posts	4 x exclusive Facebook posts
On the brand website:	On the brand website:	On the brand website:
Your logo on our 'partners page'	Your logo on our Partners page'	Your logo on our 'partners page'
Your product and URL listed in the 'get the look' section	Your product and URL listed in the 'get the look' section	Your product and URL listed in the 'get the look' section
Your logo on our weekly EDM	Your logo on our weekly EDM	1 x exclusive feature blog
		Your logo on all marketing flyers, brochures & banner
For your usage:	For your usage:	For your usage:
Usage rights to the photography	Usage rights to the photography	Usage rights to the photography
	Custom testimonial	Custom testimonial
Package value = $10,000	Package value = $20,000	Package value = $35,000

YOUR VALUE CAN BE CATEGORISED INTO A FEW DIFFERENT AREAS:

Product

If you are giving your partner product in exchange for other elements, you need to be clear about a few things.

- Is this a new product or existing product? If your product is exclusive to a retailer, you may have a restriction around where it can appear. You may be developing a custom product, for example a flavour or ingredient not available anywhere else. It could be a larger or a reduced size of the product or a limited-edition product with a mix of both brands, for example a Tim Tam flavoured Drumstick ice cream.

- How does this product need to be handled or stored so when the customer receives the product, it reflects your company in the right way? E.g. A new beverage that must be served cold to the customer when you are sampling the item at an outdoor concert.

- You must agree on the number of units and where it will be available. If there are spares, or all the product isn't given out, do you want it to be shipped back or are you happy for them to use it at another event? Do you want it given to a charity?

- Geographical reach should also be discussed. Are your products only available at your one retail location, e.g. a hairdresser based in Brisbane, but the partner has national distribution? They could be promoting your name in WA, but you aren't getting more customers in your door.

Digital deliverables

Your digital elements are just as fragile as a product. You don't want them used in areas or in a way that isn't agreed. Think about:

- Website usage. Is it a banner on your home page or an article on your blog? If it was a giveaway of your ebook, you might want a unique code so you can track how many people download it.
- Social media. Will you share footage taken on your iPhone, or will it be professional footage? How many posts? The frequency and length? Just your brand or a heap of brands? Will it include the product name, additional hashtags like #interiordesign? Will a highlight reel be done that will stay on the page? Will it appear on Instagram, YouTube, Facebook, LinkedIn, Snapchat, TikTok?
- The usage rights of the content produced need to be considered. Can your partner take the images you produce and create a brochure of their own with the shots? Can they use the image as advertising on social media?

Events or in-person experiences

Usually, events have a lot of partners involved therefore you need to assess if this is a deal you are doing just with the organiser, or a large cooperative event where you all agree to assist each partner.

- Before the event, will your logo appear on all the invitations? Are there emails that could be sent surrounding your product/service or yourself if you are the speaker? What is the frequency of the email, and the open rate and click-through rate to the website?
- The database of who attends is the most valuable asset you can gain, but the organiser must confirm this has been addressed in their privacy policy. If you don't get this, you could try to integrate the attendees' details in another way, such as encouraging them to tag you in photos from the event or scan a QR code presented on screen, at a booth or at the book signing.

- If you are part of the goodie bag that goes out to attendees, does your voucher have an expiry date or a value? Is the discount based on a minimum spend, or does it include postage? Can the code be used by friends or used several times in the promotional period?

The idea is to look at what you are willing to offer to get your desired results from this partnership. Then dig a little deeper to assess what the cost will be to your company and how your team will actually provide what's promised to your partner. The next step is to put it in writing.

HOW TO FORMALISE THE PARTNERSHIP

An agreement or deal memo is a written document where two parties agree about their rights and responsibilities. It is signed off by each party who confirm they will each execute what is required within the agreed time frame. What I mean by *Rights*, are what you are entitled to and *responsibilities* means the stuff you agree to give or do in exchange. Your diligence around documenting the deal shows you are being professional and are committed.

The two reasons you need to do this are:

1. Legally, should it go there, it needs to be defendable.
2. But more likely, enforceable by you with the other party.

Think about legal protection and its impact

Most collaborations are done via email and are quite casual. Agreeing that you will send an email to your database or tag a brand in a post doesn't need a lawyer to write a contract. Plenty of deals are agreed to over lunch and some very casually as a referral when you are asked. To make it easy for you, I am going to outline the elements worth considering in an agreement, and depending on the deal, you can decide what is relevant for your deal and judge if legal assistance is required.

The sentiment is that both of you are coming together to do something exciting and it will feel like a great opportunity. Be excited. This is a great day. You are progressing and another company feels so strongly about you that they want to align with you for the world to know you are working together. I bet when you started your company, this was a dream!

WHAT TO HAVE IN YOUR AGREEMENT

- Company name, contact person, contact email, phone number of the primary and secondary contact at each company.
- Brand name, product names plus colours/models.
- Campaign name, timing/dates, audience numbers
- Partner one obligations – what they are willing to do in as much detail as possible.
- Partner two obligations – what they are willing to do in as much detail as possible
- Restrictions of where the collaboration can be used, geographically, in print and digitally.
- An exit clause – if partner one does not deliver the agreed elements, then partner two reserves the right to claim the cost of the product delivered..

Exposure and risk

As I've mentioned, many collaborations don't have legal contracts drawn up, but of course, this should be a judgement made by you depending on the terms and the circumstance. Your *exposure* is about being unprotected and open to danger in the event of an undesirable situation. *Risk* is about assessing the probability that your company will be harmed or experience an adverse effect if things don't go to plan.

What happens if the deal does not produce the agreed return?

You need to make an assessment on how this will affect your business and what the probability will be. Only then can you decide if you should have a legal contract drawn up. Alternatively, the other party could have a standard contract and you must assess whether you want to enter into the legal agreement presented to you.

Questions to ask yourself

If you made an agreement created by both parties, and not a lawyer, and one party didn't do what they said they would, what would the implications be for your business? If a partner agreed to post on Instagram and they didn't, would you hire a lawyer to enforce it? The legal fees would be more than the benefit of getting the post. How much are you prepared to spend to argue in court?

If you were expecting the deal to add to your business growth, but it wasn't guaranteed, then that would be hard to argue legally. However, these are some of the questions to consider to get the best from the deal:

- Is there money changing hands? Is it $50,000 in cash plus product?
- Is there a significant investment being made by one or both parties? It could be you set up a new production facility, a unique fabric run or create new packaging with barcodes.
- Is there a significant retailer involved? If the deal could ruin your relationship with Target/David Jones/Bunnings for all your products and brands, then you'd want to have a legal agreement in place.
- A legal agreement would be essential if you are creating a new product, and there is a tooling, design cost or large production cost involved to create containers worth of products. This would be likely to include safety standards testing, photography, public relations agency costs or full page advertising costs in magazines.

- For a formal licensing agreement, where you are applying a brand you don't own to your product, you *must* have a legal contract.

Written deals also protect you

I cannot stress enough that you should be documenting what both parties have agreed to deliver throughout the deal period and also at the end of the campaign. If you don't value your worth, then it's almost impossible to get a company to recognise and prioritise working with you. I have seen multiple misunderstandings between companies which result in bad blood in a deal that could have been so sweet.

When I signed a licensing deal, of course Jeep was protecting their brand and ensuring I delivered on manufacturing the brand appropriately. They needed to ensure I would pay them each quarter, whether I sold one unit or a thousand. However, the other side of the deal was protecting me so they couldn't just exit the contract without penalty, or sign up another manufacturer in my region that would go against me. It's a two-way street.

Legal speak can be scary

If you're thinking your partner will think you're going over the top, change the perspective to focus on them. 'I want to ensure I deliver on everything we discussed, and should I go on holidays or get sick, then this outline lets my team know what they need to do to deliver on this deal.'

If you are given a contract by your partner, don't be scared if their legal team throws in some clauses you don't understand. You can get it looked at by your own lawyer or call your partner's lawyer and ask them to explain in detail what the statements mean.

The complexity of the contract should reflect the size of the deal and the gain you can make. The Jeep deal was worth millions of dollars, and it was four pages in total. Be fair and very clear, and if it gets too hard, trust your instinct and decide if you want to walk away. There is always another deal.

A GOOD STRUCTURE WILL DELIVER DIVIDENDS

You are creating great value and so is your partner. You are both working towards giving your mutual customer a great experience. Please let me offer you some tips that will help you in the future.

- Document as if you had to let one of your junior staff run the partnership for you and imagine you have to have three months off work. Have the detail saved in a logical place; save the emails, keep the receipts, file everything simply. Have a backup on your Google Drive too.
- Treat your partner like a customer. It's so easy to send regular updates and build the relationship. Absence of information forms doubt.
- Be clear with your staff about saving and storing images with dates and restrictions. Have a naming convention like: PartnerName-FBpost-eventintro-06092021.
- Ensure your team are also saving what the partner is creating and sharing with their audience, and store it in another folder.
- Save media clippings if they are securing press for your joint project.

Your staff need to understand why it's important that they save clearly and logically. Your team needs to easily find and access these files in the short term in order to deliver on your deal so you can assess your return on investment. Into the future, you can also show your future partners the quality of your work. There is nothing more frustrating or time consuming than searching through posts from a year ago or trawling through emails trying to find an attachment. Make it non-negotiable with your team, or better still, make it an objective for them to get their BONUS!

While we are on the topic of storage, ensure you save files on a cloud so you can access anywhere and at any time. You can also cut access if a staff member leaves or a partner's staff member goes to a competitor. Google Drive or Dropbox are known by everyone and easy to share from.

SNAPSHOT

You are building your reputation, your credibility, your assets and your long-term commerciality. You are clear on the value you have in your business and are able to construct a deal based on the value exchange. The deal memo is clear and easy for your staff or your partner's staff to access and deliver upon or consult for detail if the deal isn't being delivered. You look diligent and professional.

You are clear on the value of offering more than you ask and storing the results of the campaign along with the images, videos, testimonials, press clippings and point of sale. Trust me, you will be able to use these to your advantage more than you would expect.

The next chapter is about delivering on your deal. Putting together the campaign is the best bit. You want to ensure your customer snaps up your promotion and engages in your content.

I'll also tell you the one thing almost no-one does that will have you in the top percentage of partners straight out of the gate. It happened to me ONCE and I've told 100 companies to partner with this company because of the way they behave in a partnership.

You will become a professional machine at delivering what you said you would and the way you'll do it will impress your partner so much, they won't shut up about you.

It's the star factor! The things you do that will make you sparkle amongst an ocean of coal.

Chapter 6
GET READY TO OVER-DELIVER!

'It's not a marketer's job to tell our message to every single person. Instead, we need to find our core believers and share our message with them. The believers will then spread the message to nonbelievers and "convert" or "influence" them to become believers.' – **Seth Goodwin**

A PARTNER ECOSYSTEM IS ABOUT EXPANDING YOUR REACH AND GROWING REVENUE FOR BOTH SIDES

I want you to be at the top of the list of partners who over-deliver, so you'll be highly regarded, seen as trustworthy and the next partnership will find you! I hope you've learnt a few things along the way in this book so far, but if this chapter doesn't have you leaping out of your chair, ready to switch on your partnership mindset, then I don't know what will!

You've done the deal on paper, now it's time to execute. You've agreed to what you'll give each other, so now the soul focus should be your mutual customer and what they get from the partnership. The whole point is to create something that will appeal to them that couldn't be done by one party alone. The ultimate 1 + 1 = 3 moment.

I'm not talking about you thinking this deal is just the act of ticking boxes with no passion or purpose. I want you to feel the partnership is something you're really proud you could bring to the customer: one they will appreciate, love and tell others about.

This is the fun part

This is where you come together and get to create, engage and deliver! It's important you come from a place of generosity – you're building your business, your profile, your personal brand, your customers admiration and spend as well as your partner's advocacy.

Make it genuine. Don't copy and paste or sound like a robot. Share why you love what you've created, how the story began, the details of the discovery and the wonderful hiccups that occurred along the journey to magnificence.

As I hinted in the last chapter, I partnered with a small brand who did something so insightful and disarming that I've told their story 100 times to anyone looking for a great partnership deal. Something so simple you'll probably think I'm loopy, but the point is, the simple things don't happen *simply* in business. Most of the time, I am chasing partners to deliver what they agreed, as they fall into a ticking boxes mindset. It's uncomfortable and unnecessary.

Let's talk about the key elements to becoming magnificent

- The reverse brief – the one thing that will make you a standout and be the diamond in the coal.
- Creating content as a partner not an influencer.
- Your assets are worth money – how to save, store and share this content.
- Over-deliver! Always offer more than you ask.

THE REVERSE BRIEF

If you're thinking, *We covered what should be in the deal agreement last chapter* – then hang on. Now we are talking about a reverse brief, because it's the key element to being in the top percent. Let me summarise what a reverse brief is: it's going back to the partner with an outline of the deal with examples. NOW, let me tell you why this never happens and why it should.

Many deals are done by third parties – PR agencies, talent agencies and sometimes salespeople or business owners. They are well intentioned and I'm not detracting from their importance. However, the way you construct the campaign elements and the message to your customers is critical to its success. An account manager at an agency might not understand how to use the product in detail and may assume some critical steps. Or the salesperson who constructed a deal at the big brand may have left the company. Sometimes it can be months, or even years, between the deal being done and the campaign starting.

A reverse brief is a refresher and delivers confidence to your partner that you are operating at the highest level and clarifies what will be delivered. In the time gap, products may have been superseded, stores may have been closed, event attendance could have doubled, so give the partner the courtesy to address the deal now, clarify or slightly adjust. Allowing them to achieve what they need *now* is a luxury rarely given.

I've learnt from doing hundreds of partnerships that we are all constantly changing to suit trends, market opportunities, other partners or new retailers, so giving your partner the chance to vary their deliverables will put you in a GODLIKE position and they will remember you forever.

Be the partner who is talked about

I want you to feel confident. So often people assume everyone has the same understanding, but often there are misconnects. Clarification at this stage enables you to deliver at the highest level to give you the greatest chance to blow your ROI sky-high and gets the partner talking about you early on to others, while giving them the confidence they have made a great decision by partnering with you.

The partner who did this was The Wholesome Cook. I worked with her on a campaign to produce images with the product, which was a range of Christmas scented candles, and to create an element that would inspire and be sharable within her community, writing genuine content. She wrote a reverse brief back to me outlining her understanding of what I had asked. She included sample images of other campaigns to confirm this was the style, size, orientation and 'feel' I was after. She came up with an idea to include a delicious recipe with the same flavours as the candles and she provided an example of her writing for another product to show her writing style.

I could have fallen over backwards! This never, ever, ever happens in partnerships. I was in love with her from day one. She went on to over-deliver on my every expectation by creating a giveaway of the product with her cookbook to engage the audience and provide the brand with additional posts, while delivering more photos than was agreed too. She became the GOLD STANDARD in my eyes, and I have tried to emulate her level of professionalism in every deal I've done since then.

Generosity or just being savvy?

To be clear, I do think she was a very generous spirited woman, but I also think she was smart too. By doing a reverse brief, she ensured she didn't have to do her work twice or get it wrong. She knew she could deliver on the deal. Interestingly, when she did more, I gave more too. I over-delivered on what I said I would because she gave me the content packaged in a way that was easy for me to keep promoting our collaboration, and by doing this, she was extending her brand into another audience and increasing her chances of selling her cookbook and getting the next partnership.

Simple steps to a reverse brief

- To begin, get out the deal and put the top-line deliverables as headings on separate slides in a PowerPoint presentation, e.g. website banner, 400-word article, before and after images.

- On the slide that says 'images' find previous images from your partner's social media or your own social media that you think will illustrate the type of images you believe they want you to deliver. Some of the critical elements that can be assumed and not confirmed are if the images need to include a person's hand, face or family. If it's product imagery, should it be a flat-lay (flat on a table with other flat items) or a staged photo with a kitchen in the background. Portrait format is important for Instagram stories, but landscape images are needed for website banners.

- If you don't have a library of images you can draw from, then you grab your smartphone and take some images as a rough draft. Do a sketch of a product or share an image of an event that conveys the look and feel of what is being asked of you.

- Written forms such as an article, blog, long post or video script can include a link to other content you have created. It's important to show the content has delivered the product name, shown an understanding of how the customer can use the product or buy it, tagged the right partners and used a selection of hashtags to give it every opportunity to be shared.

It feels like double the work

If you are thinking this feels like a lot of work, you're not wrong. It's another level of input, but it also protects you from doing the work, and not meeting the expectations or guidelines, and having to do it all again. I can assure you, this makes you an Olympic-level athlete – they put in more work and that's why they are at the highest level.

When you have done this once, the second time takes half the time and after your third, it's a breeze! Of course, there are always exceptions to the rule. If a deal is straightforward, such as sharing posts or providing a giveaway for 200 goodie bags, then you don't need a reverse brief. It's for the deals where you want to shine, or the deals that have many elements that will take time, energy and resources to create what you need to deliver. Imagine if you created a product and spent money creating samples, only to discover there was a miscommunication. A reverse brief is good business.

Be aware that this detail is for the brand, not the agency representing the brand. If you have to rely on a member of staff or an agency to convey this to your partner, it could get lost in translation. That's why images and examples are a great way to show clarity and get confirmation. Sometimes, very rarely, a partner might be too busy to appreciate what you are doing. My example and my reaction might be a little over the top, but at the very least, a reverse brief shows your professionalism and safeguards you in the deal, in case what you create doesn't meet the partner's expectations.

CREATING CONTENT AS A PARTNER – NOT AN INFLUENCER

An influencer creates one great post in a way that their audience will appreciate and respond to.

Think of an influencer as putting a full-page ad in a magazine for a month. A partnership is a full campaign covering SEO, digital, social, PR, POS, trade/wholesale/distributors. A good partner gives their partner everything they need to succeed, so when they are creating the product for your mutual customer, they don't have to ask for anything.

Influencers are a great resource, and just like a full-page advertisement, they get you exposure to one audience, at one time, with one message. They are great for seasonal, short, sharp campaigns.

Partners are a trusted ally who are in deep with you, riding the waves, and will be there at the beginning, the middle and celebrating with you at the end.

Influencers promote your product and get paid for their promotion

A professional AFL player had a dream to build an amazing house for his family. Other than footy, he has a production company that produces a show on fishing and a separate audience who relate to him off the field, therefore in his new house he wanted to have an office area where he could record video and audio. To accomplish this, he needed products that would have great acoustics, providing him with high sound quality within the room, while also keeping the noise of his small children out. His builder chose a building product that would be suitable for his purpose.

In a conversation with the builder's CSR account manager, he told me about the build he was doing and the problem our product was solving for the homeowner. This resulted in me having a direct conversation with the AFL player. I tell this story, as the most authentic partnerships are actually genuine, and a situation arises where there is a benefit for two companies to work together as they were already an advocate, which allows them to tell their story in a real way.

In this style of collaboration, to be the best partner, CSR

provided a couple of points to discuss, links to the website, handles for social media, shirts for installers to wear with the brand and made it as easy as possible for the AFL player to create content across his platforms. The two brands were together at the beginning of the build and when the house was finished, and will work together in the future to tell an authentic story.

Make it easy for your partner with a 'toolkit'

To help your partner and give yourself the greatest chance of success, you should create a partner toolkit. This will be the information your partner needs but doesn't yet have, so they don't have to stop their creative process and contact you to find the information. It's essentially a cheat sheet. Here's a checklist for you:

- ✓ At the top, your contact details so they can reach out to you, not only in business hours, but after hours.
- ✓ Company and brand name with phonetic spelling so they can say the brand name on video and it won't be pronounced incorrectly.
- ✓ Website address and links to pages with your products they are talking about.
- ✓ Social handles for all your accounts plus hashtags you would like them to include.
- ✓ Locations where customers can purchase – could be online or a big retailer like Target or Bunnings.
- ✓ What you're best known for or your claim to fame. It could be an advertising campaign slogan, an award like Telstra Businesswoman of the Year or a quirky fact – like your company is run by sisters who married brothers.
- ✓ If you are Australian made or details about your production. The allure of an Italian, handmade garment is coveted more than a mass market piece.
- ✓ Product overview in BBQ conversation – in very simple

terms, what someone might hear about you at a BBQ and can be easily recalled later.

✓ Send them product, packaging/ bags or samples to hold up or point too.

✓ T-shirts for staff to wear at an event.

✓ Stickers, signage, brochures with your logo that could be in the background or foreground of any content or POS.

Don't get too worried about all these elements, the point is, you want to provide the information so it's easily available. Of course, if your brand is BIG, there are exceptions. The corporate guidelines might not allow for staff to wear another shirt, for example.

Again, you might be thinking, *This feels like hard work*, but imagine if you had the chance to be on TV, would you leave it up to the Gods, or would you hustle so you made the most of the opportunity? Don't kick yourself afterwards when they do a live video and can't pronounce your brand name or share a post with the old store address.

EVERYTHING YOU CREATE IS AN ASSET WITH A VALUE

If you were selling your company, you would have to value your business and the process is to look at everything that is valuable to a buyer. The partnerships and assets you create are worth money, and just like you would not shove $1,000 in an envelope and hide it in a box, you shouldn't be haphazard with the assets you create from your partnerships. They are worth your time and how you save, store and share this content now and in the future will give your returns.

It's also about repurposing – the other thing that most companies don't do. Your ability to find an asset, share it with media or repurpose it into another marketing campaign will deliver a return into the future.

Process is priceless

It's so easy to be a little lazy, but creating procedures with your staff at the beginning, including folders and systems, will assist both you and your partner. It's important you deliver the assets through a medium the partner can access e.g. Dropbox or Google Drive. It's also worth having a naming convention, such as: 2021_CSR_Three Birds_House13_productname_video. Imagine if you had the chance to be on the news tonight and the journalist needed images from you in the next twenty minutes. You need to be able to quickly share the files with your partner and other agencies, magazines or retailers, even if a year has passed and it's not fresh in your mind anymore.

Sadly, staff leave companies and sometimes the asset leaves too

All too often when staff leave, no-one can put their hands on a file anymore. Or they may still be in the company, but nobody knows where they were saved. These assets are valuable and should be treated as such. Cloud-based drives allow you to see assets on the move and gain access when and where you need it. I guarantee, three years from now, you'll go looking for that image for an idea, partner pitch, retailer pitch etc. and it will send you insane when you can't find it.

I've seen this happen in every company, and after consulting to big brands it's something I feel very strongly about. So often files sit with external agencies and the brands only receive the final PDF version of the brochure. They don't have the source files that contain the fonts, colours, layout, images and copy. Two years later, the product code is changed and the brochure needs to be updated, leaving you in a situation where you have to go back to the agency and pay them to make the change, or sadly, the file is gone and you have to pay a new agency to create a whole new brochure, costing you time and money.

Set up a share drive right now

- Set up a folder called partnerships.
- Sub-folders for each partner.
- Save all files – deal, brand tool kit, costs, images, videos, articles, press.
- Set up folders for products you create together.

It's really important you both use the share folders to collaborate on documents while they are being developed. Ensure you are both editors, but also make a copy on your own drive – just in case. Through innocence or malice, files get deleted, staff take files and go to competitors, disagreements arise or divorce occurs. Ensure you are ready for any circumstance with a well set up share drive and also take backups of those folders.

You will want to use them in the future to show to new prospective partners, but mostly you want to continue to use the assets in different formats and different stages of your business. If this all sounds boring, like advice your accountant would give you, I promise you will be crying if something happens and you don't have a copy.

TIME TO OVER-DELIVER ON YOUR DEAL

Thank goodness! It's agreed to and now you can concentrate on doing the fun stuff – actually executing all the great marketing elements and the campaign you've dreamed off. Roll up your sleeves and start over-delivering with enthusiasm and generosity.

There are three stages to over-delivering on the deal:

1. Working on the elements well before you launch so your partner is congratulating themselves on choosing such a diligent partner.
2. The campaign itself is when the message goes to market

and you become the dream partner who is inclusive and over-communicates.

3. The encore – the time when you come back and show what a good job you've done, so they can tell the whole industry how impressive you are.

Working on the campaign

Go to your agreement and begin by executing who is going to create what and by when. Do you need their logo, next season's colours, style guides, fabric patterns, new formula or recipes? Be realistic about time frames – you might have to use an outside agency to do the creative and then go back to your partner for approval.

The most critical element at this phase is to be crystal clear about what is going on. Get their approval at different points of the process so there are no surprises. You must have everything ready to go when the date arrives to launch your campaign.

It should be in your agreement but here are some things to think about in the creative stage:

- Article length or number of words, plus the number of mentions with backlinks to their website.
- Photography brief detail, including styled or behind the scenes images, blurred people walking or in-focus people, orientation and space around subject. This is important as space around a subject might be a critical detail when you come to create a landscape banner for the webpage and need an area to lay text on the image without going over the hero product.
- Teaser emails for an event should include links, logos and images.

Campaign go-live date

Again, go back to what was agreed, but this is the time when I want you to over-deliver on their expectations and the actual 'deliverables'. My pet hate is having to tick off the deliverables like a checklist and go back on the last day and tell the partner they haven't done something they agreed to.

At this stage, an extra post or extra story on Instagram will show you want to do everything you can to make the deal work. It's the little extras that don't cost you anything that add up to tipping the campaign into a complete success.

Have you thought about:

- Posting the article on your webpage, social stories, LinkedIn profile of the company and also your own private accounts?
- Saving the video from the IGTV so you can give them the original footage for their library.
- Sharing the event attendees' database in a format that includes extra fields such as their Instagram account handle or whether they are a buying customer or a prospect.
- The photography is so important. Give them a few more images than you agreed to. If you have images with a celebrity or talent that can't be used by them, make it clear, but perhaps give it to them as a souvenir. See if you can blur any people or give them the shots where the person is not recognisable such as the back of their head or them walking down a hallway.
- Usage rights may have been agreed to for six months, but you could give them an extra few weeks or maybe until the end of the calendar year. This also applies to the logo. With Three Birds Renovations, one of their partners continues to use the house in their advertising but can only type the partner's name in the ad, not use the logo or the image of the three girls.
- Sometimes usage rights may be the medium, for example, they can only be used on digital platforms. You could give them one image you love in high resolution and allow to use it in print for six months, which allows them to include

it in a catalogue or brochure. This is of benefit to you too as they keep extending your brand.

- You don't have to give away everything, but show the assets you have. They might offer something in exchange e.g. extra EDM for another six images.
- Social shares are the easiest to give away but can also give you the benefit of ROI. If you did an extra post valued at $800 and engaged an audience of 3,000 people, you can demonstrate that their investment was $0 and the ROI goes from 10:1 to 25:1.

I did a collaboration with Network Ten's *The Living Room* program and over-delivered by providing more images of a promotion with their audience. They used those images to secure editorial in *TV Week* magazine and the story generated thousands of website hits to the ecommerce site I was working with. Generosity seems to come back tenfold.

Give without wanting something in return

Human nature is that you might feel like you want to ask them for something. Try to resist. In most cases, your generosity will come back to you. Or perhaps you are feeling like you'll look desperate if you give away too much, devaluing your own brand. I'm not suggesting for one moment that you give away the farm. I want you to be the brand at the top of the list and showing gratitude and eagerness will only make you a more attractive partner. Have a long-term view.

Golden ticket to future partnerships

The biggest tip I can give when you are in the campaign phase is to keep communicating. Most partners check everything off but don't share the success along the way. You don't have to give away the best bits, but sending them a fortnightly or monthly email with just a few highlights keeps them highly engaged. It could be small wins, like episode views have gone over 10,000, after the first week of the competition you have over 5,000 entries or a post you have done with over 1,000 likes.

Regardless of your partner's size, they want to share your compatibility and your wins with their stakeholders. Many corporate marketing managers have monthly reports that need to be done. Giving them information they can share shows your success and helps them to substantiate that the deal was a good one. When you demonstrate access to a much wider audience, your brand is a partner they will want to deal with again. You wouldn't leave your best girlfriend at a bar on her own, so don't let your partner hang out wondering. Keep them up to date.

If your campaign isn't delivering, don't lie. Providing them with figures or percentages that are creative at best, or flat-out fabrication, is going to burn both of you in the long run. However, you can find the rose amongst the thorns and be selective about sharing the best figures you have.

Be specific

You want to be specific so there are no grey areas. If your partner asks for something extra you can't deliver, try to give a little something that is possible. At every stage, you want to measure the campaign statistics and pivot slightly in order to get the best performance you can. Happy partners tell others how great you were and give examples of how professional you act. This adds to your credibility and your ability to get the next deal. No brand wants to deal with a hack! Don't forget, agencies sometimes represent multiple talents. Your reputation will precede you, and if your partners rave about you, it gives the agent confidence to recommend you instead of someone else.

If you're thinking they will get sick of you contacting them, you're wrong. In many deals there is often radio silence and it's the partner emailing and calling for an update. At this stage, you don't need to document every detail, just the main headlines. Keep it simple: always put the customer at the centre of your decision-making and reporting. What did they gain? How is your brand helping your partner look better in the eyes of the customer?

SNAPSHOT

You can see how a few tweaks to a process can have you going from pedestrian to pop star. Creating the product for your mutual customer will drive the outcomes you set out for. If you have a partnership mindset, go the extra mile and do the reverse brief to cement yourself as the GOLD STANDARD.

Remember that the deal memo had a perceived value exchange – you both agreed to invest in the partnership to create a campaign and assets that would drive buyer behaviour. The perceived value becomes tangible when you get access to the assets. This value transfers to the assets then. Keep them safe, saved, stored logically and with sharing rights restricted but able to be shared in a second if it could lead to the next partnership.

The only barrier you need to overcome is creating a procedure, sharing the procedure with your staff and monitoring the access into the shared file. I want you to feel confident you are developing a partnership marketing mindset that will elevate you above your competitors and make you an ally for businesses you want to deal with.

You've done the deal, and you're delivering on it. Just like an elite athlete, what extra training could you do to extend your reach even further? I'm going to give you extra ways to leverage your partnership and give you currency in other areas of your business.

In the next chapter we uncover how to use your partnership to cement your brand's innovation and leadership in the eyes of your retailers, suppliers, industry associations and colleagues. Become the brand your competitors talk about, not just customers.

Chapter 7
PLAY THE BIGGER GAME AND SHARE THE LOVE

ALLIANCES OPEN UP CREATIVE WAYS TO ACHIEVE CUSTOMER SATISFACTION THAT AREN'T POSSIBLE WHEN BRANDS OPERATE INDEPENDENTLY

So far we have looked at how to find and work with your preferred partner, structure the deal and then over-deliver on your partners expectations. It's a very simple recipe for success. Now I want to illustrate how you can extend this deal to over-deliver for your **own brand.**

I want you to play the bigger game and learn from the big brands. It's about extending your reach and sharing the love to media, industry groups, installers or tradies and your retailers.

When you amplify your partnership you are doing it because others can benefit. It creates a talking point, increased credibility, the chance of additional sales and increased brand reach. Of course, you want the world to know, but think of it from the point of view of the receiver of the news. I'm not talking about blatant sales broadcasting here – they 'won't care'. Talk about why it *matters* to them. Share the *why* in the conversation.

This is all about repurposing those beautiful videos, photos and content pieces you've worked on together with your partner to extend your reach and establish yourself as a business worth collaborating with. Share the news within your industry and to the relevant media, who are always looking for good news stories. It's also good business to share your little wins along the way with your partner – they'll love a juicy love story. Use the partnership to show your retailers your talents and give them a story to tell *their* customers.

Share with stakeholders

You want to be a great partner, that's a given, but the communications you have created are aimed at your mutual customer, not other stakeholders in your brand. It's just one extra step to share with other stakeholders and establishes your profile, providing credibility and trust.

Each year, CSR create an awards campaign to recognise and reward the best Gyprockers – the craftsmen who install plasterboard and turn projects into works of art. We partner with suppliers such as Intex, Wallboard and Makita, as our tradies need their tools to do the job. The winner receives prizes, plus the title of the CSR Gyprocker of the Year. We happily share the winners' projects, stories and images with the building industry media, and glossy home media.

It's all about showing that these exceptional tradies are true craftsmen, and as the best in their industry, they use the best products in the industry – namely CSR Gyprock. When one of our winners are then profiled in the media, we are proud to see their name in lights. We know other tradies will want to elevate their brand name and projects, showing the standard they have to achieve, which includes using a quality product like CSR Gyprock. Receiving media for the winners is icing on the cake and makes us a better partner.

In this chapter, I will show you who to share the fruits of

your partnership with in your industry, how to use it to assist your retailers and also how to package and share it back to your partner so they can see the increased level of support you are creating to over-deliver in a totally new way.

ELEVATE YOUR PROFESSIONAL PROFILE

I want you to talk to the media, your industry associations and networking groups about your partnership. Remember communication is all about talking in a language your target audience understands and will make them act. Leadership is about showing others the path to evolve and grow. You are helping others when you share your story.

Share with consumer media

- Create a case study or story about the campaign or something you found out. Focus on the most enticing angle and understand the case study may only be 5% about your brand. It may highlight a problem a customer had and how your partnership campaign created the solution.
- Take the hero element – *Five top ways to nail the beach boho vibe in your house.* What you have created is one of the top five ways.
- Printed home magazines will be interested in exclusives and tours, whereas digital media will love something different. For example, Homestolove.com.au – which is about speed to market and lots of articles.
- Newspapers syndicate articles all the time, one story can appear in 130 regional papers. These are short articles but are great if you have a statewide or online presence.

Professional media are your influencers in the industry

- Architects and interior designers love being covered in consumer magazines, but also industry publications to show peers their success. This is the same for human resources, software creators, hairdressers, chefs – any professional service provider. Each service needs tools and these are likely to be products.
- Industry publications like seeing who is active and what they are achieving. B&T are prolific in the advertising industry for elevating agencies who create groundbreaking campaigns.
- Industry likes to see new ways to use products beyond the traditional application.
- Take a look at the stories being published and find a common thread or way to promote your partnership. Are you solving an industry problem?

Trade media – show the how-to version

- People who install your product like seeing what's new. Or a new way to tie a belt, ice a cake, make a cocktail.
- New ideas give them conversation with their peers and colleagues.
- When you post on social, other creators may provide ways they have done it, to show what else is possible. Again, this could be about social media implementation, how to design an online course, how to create a grazing platter. It's showing the work in action.

Industry media can identify you as a reliable source

- Manufacturers' magazines, gift and homeware associations, licensing, marketing/business publications – whatever is relevant to you.
- Your ambition here is to show how you are progressing in your industry.
- This also illustrates you are the go-to person for the next opportunity or to provide a comment or story.

Networking groups are advocates

- Whether it's Business Chicks, Like Minded Bitches Drinking Wine or your rotary/local council group, share what you are doing with your partnership. It helps others to think of ways to do this in their business.
- Your local council will feed the local newspaper with story ideas.
- Share your joy! Not only will it spark people's interest in your brand, but your status will be elevated.
- This could also be an opportunity for you to be asked to speak at an industry event or be on a podcast.
- These supporters want you to succeed and may not be your target market, but they will share your story with their tribe.

TAKE EVERY OPPORTUNITY PRESENTED TO YOU

The purpose of a partnership is to achieve a marketing objective linked to your target customer by joining forces with a like-minded company. However, it can also make you an attractive partner for other companies as it illustrates your professionalism, then your stock rises.

As mentioned, this is an extension task. You don't have to do this, but you've already done the hard work, so this extra step is about getting a little glory and elevating your profile.

A great example of this is the marketing industry media. Advertising agencies submit stories about the campaigns they create and the results their clients achieved. Some corporate marketing professionals read the industry media, but it's likely to be other agency staff reading these publications. Their peers can see which agencies they want to partner with, refer to clients, discover who might be a takeover target and also read how they created the campaigns so they can learn themselves.

I did a collaboration deal with Kyal and Kara from *The Block* 2016 who were building their new house. After the partnership was completed, I wrote a press release from a building products' perspective with a look into their home. It was picked up by assorted digital media across the country and this one piece of work gained over $100,000 in media coverage for the brands I was working with.

As podcasts are the fastest growing medium in 2021, I also believe you should aim to be on as many podcasts as possible. The strength of this style of media is that it is a long format, so listeners hear your voice, your story and your personality and make a connection with you. The number of times I have listened to a podcast and immediately gone to the website of the guest to buy their service is very high. I feel like they are talking straight to me about how they could solve a problem I have.

Share a media release

If you don't know how to write a media release you can find templates to follow online. The most important is to put the five Ws in the first paragraph – who, what, where, when and why – and keep it under a page. Ensure you have a link to Dropbox for images. If you don't provide images, you won't get published.

There are whole books written on public relations, so you can do this yourself. The alternative is to go to freelancer.com and pay a writer to edit your version of the press release to ensure it's perfect. Some freelancers will also send it to their media contacts on your behalf, with your contact details in case journalists need more information. The most important aspect of this is to follow up with the media you sent it to. If you have created a product from your partnership collaboration, you could send them the product as well or offer them a link to download the digital product.

Please remember that you tailor the media release to the audience of the magazine. Announce what's in it for the customer or why this is groundbreaking for the industry, where they can get the product and which retailers are supporting the campaign. If you don't get published you can still use the media release on your website and socials, tagging in relevant industry, groups and media – nothing is wasted.

USE YOUR PARTNERSHIP TO HELP YOUR RETAILERS

Your retailers, stockists, distributors, wholesalers, resellers, installers or anybody who buys your product and then sells it onto a third party are your immediate customers and they are your number one priority. They are your partnerships that are always on. Think about how you can repurpose the collaboration campaign elements you created to share with your stockists and help them close a deal.

Let's discuss the type and style of stockists:

- The big guys – Bunnings, Target, Woolworths.
- Specialised chain – Repco, Baby Bunting, Rebel Sport, Priceline.
- Independent – specialty stores like clothing, homewares,

barbeque or jewellery that are owned by a small business owner.

- Independent service-based businesses – architects, interior designers, artisan bakers.
- Bespoke – eco/green, paleo food, antiques
- Ecommerce-only stockists.
- Distributors, wholesalers and resellers could be interstate or overseas and sell your product to retailers.
- Installers or creators use your product to sell the solution to your customer. .

Share your marketing collateral

You've invested in the partnership, and you want the best return on your investment. The marketing should be shared widely to assist in the whole chain to the end customer. Remember in chapter five when we were negotiating the deal, there may have been restrictions that the partner imposed. Please check these before you start distributing. You need approval to use your partner's logo on anything that wasn't agreed to, however this could also be a great extension for your partner so it's likely they will welcome the opportunity.

Perfect example of leverage

TH Brown is an astute manufacturer and owner of finely crafted bespoke furniture. Their style is reminiscent of the mid-century modern style of the 1960s, and like Parker, their original pieces have become collectors' editions selling for thousands of dollars. In 2018, the family were able to get the manufacturing rights back that had been sold in the 1980s enabling them to recreate the classic pieces and sell to the next generation of homeowners who appreciate the style and the quality of this Australian-made and owned brand.

To assist their marketing, they requested the retailer fill in a customer profile when they become a stockist. This helped them to create tailored marketing collateral that would assist the retailer to sell their products instore.

Some of the point-of-sale collateral they have prepared includes the Australian-made manufacturing story, their brand heritage and trust, with the original owner's grandson as the figurehead of the company. They show the images of homes where their products have been used and interior designers they have partnered with, who have photographed and ensured they are credited. It also helps to name-drop these professionals, along with the names of celebrities who have purchased their products.

As they continue to form collaborations with leading brands, they continue to communicate with their retailers to take them along on their skyrocketing success. In 2021, the TH Brown kitchen stool was chosen by Mitch and Mark, contestants on *The Block*. The retailers feel part of their journey and can proudly advocate on their behalf, which assists in the ultimate goal of selling to customers and placing orders with TH Brown.

What different stockists need from partnerships

What ecommerce want is different to what retail stores require, but here's a list to get you thinking about how you can create collateral to assist your stockists to sell:

- Your partnership product could become a catalogue special in the Big W baby week promotion.
- Create point of sale that fits with the retail environment – it could be a poster, a flyer used on table in a restaurant or a sign that hangs from a shelf instore.
- Brochures/flyers that can be handed to customers.
- Images that can be used with the product on a digital sales page, showing the product in a lifestyle environment like a home or a dress being worn at a restaurant.
- A flyer that goes out with samples. TileCloud sell five

samples for $15, but there could be a postcard showing the use with an offer to download a reno checklist – free of charge. Or an offer on bathroom taps.

- They could bundle your product with another leading brand in store. This allows independent retailers to create a bespoke purchase to get them up to another price point with a sale.
- Your digital product would be a gift with purchase incentive – buy and get a designers' guide to styling or a ten-visit pass to a local yoga studio.
- Ecommerce stockists might want digital assets like a ten-second video to share with their audience on IGTV.
- It could be part of a digital library that is created for season product releases containing new products, packaging, styled images and short copy, all with instructions on how it could be used in an email or on socials.
- An article about it being locally made to give a focus on uniqueness that is customised to show the state, local artisan (meet Rachael), details about the source materials (e.g. Farmer Dan grows the apples for our muesli).

Use your partnership to get new retailers onboard

To boost your chances of gaining a new stockist, use your partnership videos and story in your sales kit to give retailers confidence in your brand. You could add a page or flyer in your physical pack or add a slide into your PowerPoint deck outlining your partnerships, to gain credibility and trust.

A little extra incentive could be a new range to be released: customers can pre-order but only with retailers who are onboard by a certain time frame. They need to sign up now, or they will miss out.

Perhaps you are thinking that your retailer might see this as competition. It could also have the effect of sparking a conversation about you creating a product with that retailer exclusively.

Most will see the partnership as you elevating the profile of the brand and making their job easier to sell your product.

SHARE LITTLE WINS ALONG THE WAY – THEY LOVE A JUICY LOVE STORY

When you are working in larger partnerships, you can sometimes feel like a tiny part of a large campaign. Or sometimes it is a long, long journey taking years until you reach the finish line. The advice I want to share is that you share the wins along the way and those of your partners. We will cover the wrap-up of the campaign later in the book, but I want to encourage you to share as much information and little wins along the journey of the partnership as possible. Such a simple thing will make you head and shoulders above the competition.

Consider your partner as important as the customer. You want them to rave about you. If you are part of a series that will air on YouTube, share the schedule of when you are going to air with the dates and exact times, and when their brand will appear in the episodes. If you can do this weeks or months in advance, it will help you, as they will probably elevate the episode with Facebook ad support.

Share a regular email with your entire group of partners to get them excited about the campaign before it starts and let them know at a high level what to watch for. For example, 'Here's a peek at our Facebook ads you might see over the next six weeks.'

Once the first elements have been aired to your mutual customer, share the love of how it's going. You don't have to share exact metrics but share every little win. Things like:

- People from all over the world viewed the YouTube clip – even in Spain!
- We hoped to get 1,000 views over the whole campaign, and we've already met that target.

- We've already sold out of one item after only seven days.
- We've been picked up by the media and the campaign will appear in *Home Beautiful* in October.
- Shhh! Celebrity who's a bit of a REBEL just bought our product.

The point of this is to keep them excited, as excitement will help them propel the campaign with their audience. If they feel they aren't valued and are just a worthless addition to your campaign, there will only be resentment. One idea is to create an IGTV channel of all the times you mentioned a client. They love that! Keeping all the assets you created, plus editorials, will help you when you create the partner return on investment pack, which we will cover later in the book.

Feeling forgotten

As a partner who has been forgotten and treated poorly many, many times, I know the feeling of being devalued. There is always a bigger fish, but you can make everyone feel special just by including them in the campaign hype. If you are dealing with larger companies, remember their marketing staff have to walk into management meetings each week/month and report on their campaigns. It makes them look stupid when they don't have anything to report. I always used to say jokingly to agencies, 'Your job is to make me look good.' The point being, it makes your partner look stupid when they don't know anything about the campaign, and I can guarantee they will tell colleagues how they felt.

I have partnered with a brand on the rise in the media space and they have become successful and the media now flock to them. Previously, they would have been over the moon to secure even one piece of editorial. Their business relies on many partners contributing to their projects, with free product and also a significant cash payment for sponsorship. They sign deals about two years in advance and then you feel 'forgotten' until one of their staff wants to order the product. The project takes another year and then the campaign is developed after that. I was constantly in the dark and only contacted when it suited them. Once the campaign was live, the hype was huge and once again partners were shut out of the campaign glow. If I asked about the performance, I was given metrics and visibility four to six months after the campaign.

Speaking with other partners, I know I'm not the only person who felt undervalued. Even partners who had invested twice as much were disregarded. They eventually get in contact to show a report, but it felt like a sales pitch to got you onboard for the next project and the report was only about how they benefitted, with an assumption that since they did, you did too.

Not once have they asked what success I saw from being a partner or what they could do to assist me. They have become a big fish now.

It's easy to be inclusive

The moral of the story above is that if you are excited, they will be too. If you think your metrics are too small to be impressive, then share other highlights or comments you have received on socials asking about their brand. All metrics can be presented to seem impressive – use percentages instead of actual numbers and use comments as testimonials. A quick screenshot of your post where a customer is saying how much they love your partner's products will not only bring a smile to their face, but is a thoughtful gesture to show you are as excited as them to see their success.

Treat your partners as you would like to be treated. Be inclusive and genuine and give them a trail of breadcrumbs to follow throughout the campaign. They will be your vocal advocates. I'm not telling you to share every detail, that's the big reveal at the end. My experience has been that being part of a large partnership with many brands can feel quite lonely. It's a generous-spirited thing to feel part of something special. Ultimately, people will forget what you said and did, but they will remember how you made them feel.

SNAPSHOT

We've all been the one left out from a party at some stage. The feeling you give others when you are generous of spirit will live on long after the metrics are forgotten. Being inclusive and sharing while the partnership campaign is in progress will allow your stakeholders to enjoy the progress, and the feeling is infectious. The by-product of this inclusion is extending the branding, conversations, marketing and sales opportunities for everyone in your wider circle.

The only thing you need to ensure is that after you have drawn up your partnership deal, think of all the ways you can include others. Of course, your costs may increase if you are printing material for your stores, but look at it as a sales investment to get more orders. I want you to feel strong in the belief that others want to be part of your journey and will sing about your success. If they are included, they are more willing to support you in other areas of your business.

In the next chapter, we are going to wrap up the campaign with such a beautiful bow that your next partnership will fall out of the sky. You've finished the campaign and now you want to pull together all the findings. The aim of this is to discover and learn where the success was for your company and your partner, and create a case study so compelling it becomes your pitch to get the next partnership.

Chapter 8
THAT'S A WRAP!

'Entrepreneurs have a natural inclination to go it alone. While this do-it-yourself spirit can help you move forward, adding an element of collaboration into the mix can make you unstoppable.' – **Leah Busque**

You've finished your first partnership deal. Congratulations!! You should be really proud that you were able to establish a relationship with a partner you wanted to work with, identify what you wanted to achieve from the partnership, negotiated the deal and delivered on what you agreed on. That's a great achievement. Now that you have completed the requirements and you've both promoted the work you collaborated on, it's time to look at what you achieved and report back.

It's also really important to examine the proof of the partnership while it's still fresh so you can discover what worked, why it worked and how you can emulate it again.

Plus, in your partnership, like any relationship, it's important to communicate and find out from them what worked and why. As brands we are always looking for advocacy. We want people to talk about us at a BBQ, introduce us to others, and expand our network.

LET'S BE REAL ABOUT THIS

It was a marketing partnership and you had goals you wanted to achieve. Making friends is nice, but you could have just gone to dinner instead. You need to understand what happened in metrics, display your professionalism by showing them the facts and ask for their advocacy.

As an analogy, think of a time when you've met up with new friends from work and decided on a date and restaurant. You have a brilliant night and discover lots of great things you have in common. You enjoyed each other's company and left feeling great. The next day, you get a text saying how much they enjoyed the night and you should do it again. That emotional connection and feeling of pride that you did okay, and you'll get to do it again, that's the feeling you want to leave your partner with. You valued their time and cared enough to show them. Imagine the same situation and you didn't hear from those new friends for three months. You'd be left wondering if they really did like you and it would feel awkward to contact them again since you were left high and dry.

Each time a partner and myself come together to examine what the partnership has done, it has left such a great impression of the brand in my mind, but also leaves the door wide open to do other campaigns together in the future, or even throw an idea out there now and again. Or ask for a referral.

In this chapter we are going to cover:

- What a campaign summary or success pack looks like and what to include.
- What metrics to show that actually matter to your partner
- Showing a ROI for the campaign partnership.
- Gaining the metrics from your partner to get the whole picture.

- Finding the learnings from the project so you both can advance.
- Getting the advocacy and a testimonial.

CREATE A POST-CAMPAIGN SUCCESS PRESENTATION TO DEMONSTRATE THE VALUE OF YOUR PARTNERSHIP

A campaign success presentation can be a Word document or PowerPoint presentation that illustrates the campaign elements and metrics. You are doing this because most partners just walk away at the end and miss out on getting advocacy from the partner in the longer term. I have done many partnerships where it ended and I wasn't given any facts to know if the partner delivered on the deal or if the metrics showed whether it was a success.

REPORT THE DELIVERABLES

Create the blank template and mark on each page the things you agreed to create and share with your audiences. Don't get too worried about the template. The main point of creating a success pack is for you to show your partner that you delivered everything you agreed to, and in fact, you over-delivered on the partnership. The pack clearly outlines the assets that were created and how your audience engaged with their brand and products.

Kyal and Kara, former *The Block* contestants, created a success pack for their partners to show how the deal they did with suppliers and sponsors was over-delivered by 400%. In their pitch pack they showed an estimated 100,000 would view their series, and the actual views achieved were more than one million!! That's really impressive but it also shows the suppliers they were smart to make that deal based on the 100,000 number.

From your deal agreement, outline on each slide what the deliverable was. For example, two Instagram stories, you embed the video or screenshot the video and place it into the success pack. Underneath the asset, you document the date it ran, the Instagram account handle, the engagement rate, number of views and number of shares, plus any comments that illustrate their brand was well received – OMG I love those curtains. I want them for my house.

If you didn't do something that was agreed upon, outline why it wasn't done and how you delivered something else. I want to be really clear about this – only one in every hundred partners actually go back and debrief on the campaign success. A brand exhibiting this professional level of behaviour *will* get the next deal.

SHOW THEM A RETURN ON THEIR INVESTMENT

We all spend too much time on marketing activities that don't work. Measuring the metrics demonstrates how successful the partnership was. In the Kyal and Kara pack, they used the costs from their media kit to demonstrate what the partner would have paid in dollars to get the promotion. They then showed the return on investment:

Supplier X gave us $20,000 worth of product. We delivered over $800,000 worth of media and audience engagement.

You calculate this like so: 800,000 divided by 20,000 = a ROI of 40:1.

You could also show other metrics instead of ROI, such as clicks-throughs to their sales page. If it were an event, you could share testimonials or feedback from customers. The number of attendees and the post event survey, where 95% of people said they would come back next year because of the quality of the speakers. It could be a warranty card to show how impressed the customers were with your joint product.

The main objective is to show that there was a change in traffic, behaviour or sentiment. It's like a school report card where they show class interaction, homework participation and exams, plus comments from teachers. You want to see your effort has produced a result.

You don't have to include dollar figures at all. However, if you want to include them and don't have media rates for creating content or advertising on your website, then you can use websites like theright.fit or Tribe and look for content creatives similar to your profile to get these figures. Your partner did the deal with you because they wanted an association. Be proud of what you achieved even if the metrics are lower than you expected.

THE SUCCESS PACK WILL HOOK YOUR NEXT POTENTIAL PARTNER

Having a success pack confirms you can act on a deal and deliver, and it gains trust from the next potential partner that you will deliver again. It's hard to argue with evidence. It's also hard to resist a deal where you can gain a whole new audience without cash. Whenever I meet with partners and they show me what they delivered for other companies, it immediately elevates their attractiveness.

Once the success pack is done, you just have to rename it a 'Case Study/Project Partner'. You can alter the figures if these are confidential and instead change to a percentage. Instead of 8,000 engagement rate, you could say 20% audience engagement. If you have doubts about some of your content, or have something that didn't work, you can leave it out of the case study. Alternatively, you can do a simple one-page Partnership highlights summary.

GETTING THE METRICS FROM YOUR PARTNER WILL PROVIDE YOU WITH INVALUABLE INSIGHT AND VALUE

You have shown your partner how you delivered on the deal, so it's important to find out what was a success in their eyes. Gaining information about the aspects they loved and also where you can improve will help you grow your business.

When I do deals with larger companies, I always arrange a post-campaign meeting and ask questions. This alone has seen me be invited back the following year. Set up a meeting and have a full list of questions you want to ask. Alternatively, you could set an agenda in advance so they are prepared with the metrics or the feedback you are seeking. Don't be shy about asking for this meeting. It shows you value their feedback.

Firstly, ask them about how their audience responded with metrics

The more detail you can gain about their audience, the stronger your insight will be. This allows you to market to a similar persona or locality. If the content you created for your partner's audience had a strong engagement rate, there is a high chance they will want to work with you over and over again.

We were approached by a couple who built homes in Brisbane called Zou Build. They had a small audience but they were highly engaged and connected well with families in Queensland who recognised a similar style of home that could be renovated. They constantly created content, tagging our brand each time, and produced more than the deal prescribed. At the end of the campaign, along with sharing all the images and videos, they shared their metrics for their audience engagement. This showed me they had a strong connection with a local audience, the type of content that was engaging with our mutual customer and they had a strong desire to do more partnership projects in the future.

Ask your partner detailed questions

What you are requesting is similar to the information you illustrated for them in the success pack. You want to ask them for:

1. Which posts and type of content had the highest engagement rate with their audience. Was it a post with before and after images or a video showing how to use the product?
2. If there were multiple posts with high engagement, which product did their audience connect to the most, based on engagement rate and comments or questions on social.
3. If it had a click-through to buy a product, which products got the highest click-through rate and which product got the highest sales?
4. Questions their customers asked about your products via social, their website or through the customer service channels and for any comments that mentioned your product.
5. Which medium had the best engagement rate with their audience? Was it YouTube or Facebook?

Understand what is confidential

Be up-front about wanting their metrics to help you with your business, but also respect their confidentiality and gain a CLEAR understanding of which information can be shared and where. They may be open to you using the figures in a case study, but not sharing any of their figures in podcasts, media releases and social media. At this stage, you can ask them if you can use a ballpark or generalised statement like 'more than half', or 'doubled their sales during the period'. If they verbally tell you these insights and you agree where you can use them, it's wise to send an email with the numbers documented as a follow-up.

ASK THEM WHAT THEY LEARNT AND WHAT THEY'D DO DIFFERENTLY NEXT TIME

Partners will summarise what the outcomes were, and these will be the GOLD you can leverage and extend into your business. They will also probably share what else you could do together.

On *The Block* with Nine Network, suppliers usually create branded jackets and shirts for the contestants. However, the producers ensure that each brand gets a turn so you don't see your brand on TV very often. The marketing team did observe that the tradies were in the shots and the next year, suppliers started producing merchandise for the tradies, so their brand could be seen in the background resulting in more airtime.

Even if the partner was disappointed with an element of the campaign, such as a stock shortage in certain states or that you pronounced the name of the product incorrectly, then it's still something you can learn from for future deals. If that's the case, you could also offer to post some extra content on socials or re-share some of their content. It's just a show of good faith.

Before you close the partnership for this campaign, ask for a testimonial

If they are willing to say something positive about your partnership, then grab it!! It could be about the product you created for them or generally how you worked together. Of course, you will credit them, and this becomes an asset you can use everywhere in your business. Clarify how you can use their name, title, company name and their logo.

CSR produce a technical resource for the building industry called the *Red Book*. A prestigious architect firm said it is 'a bible for the industry'. Their credibility, coupled with the CSR brand history and size, enabled it to become a headline in media articles and that title was adopted by hundreds of other professionals from that point on.

If you are meeting in person, this is the best time to ask for a testimonial. You're looking for just a sentence or two that summarises why your company is a good choice for a partner. If they want to think about it, that's okay. You can follow up with an email, but it's nicer to ask in person. Be careful about where you use it and that it's used in its entirety. Just quoting the company name could be misleading or out of context.

I understand this may feel uncomfortable – kind of like asking if they really like you, but while the partnership is still strong in their mind, it's better to ask and you will benefit in the future by having this asset in your company.

SNAPSHOT

You have learnt why it's so important to do a campaign review and create a success pack for your partner, as well as for your own benefit. What you learn is the GOLD you can take forward into other projects and by doing this pack you are showing your professionalism, creating an emotional partnership and a strong advocate for your brand.

Having confidence in what you have created for the partnership is paramount. You must never think your numbers are too small or insignificant. It could be your partner got the most value out of some feedback from your customers that allowed them to expand into an area or create a product they wouldn't have thought about. You must also find your own insights into how you can improve your brand, sales or communications.

Now that you know how to create a success pack and find the metrics and learnings, you now have a valuable asset for your business to enable you to approach your next partner with confidence and learnings you didn't have before. I'd say that's SUCCESS!

In the last chapter, you will uncover and maximise the learnings you have gained, and how to use them to advance your business. Now that you understand the value of partnerships, I'm also going to teach you how to have an 'always on marketing partnerships' mindset that will attract new partners and make you attractive to them.

Chapter 9
TAKE THE LEARNINGS AND GROW

With your newly created success pack you can really see the value of building partnerships with companies who share a similar customer to yours. Clearly, the relationship and networking value is hard to put a value on, but will be an asset for your company long-term.

Besides the relationship, the metrics have shown you in detail what customers are interested in, so you can imbed this knowledge to improve your product development and sales strategy.

The greatest gain, however, is for you to realise the advantages you can gain from partnerships and therefore recognise partnership possibilities for your business into the future.

It's important to capitalise on the knowledge you have learnt and apply it. You also need to position yourself where other companies are attracted to you as a partner. Show them your taxi light is on!

While I was working with Network Ten, *The Living Room* once spoke about how Oprah had given everyone in her audience a car – famous line: 'You get a car! You get a car!' I recognised the opportunity to partner them with an online retailer. As with many retailers, the Christmas period is when a company can make up to 70% of their annual revenue, so it's important to find a unique way to capture the attention of shoppers.

The idea was to create a Christmas episode with a twist. A live studio audience was recruited, with the help of many charities who were asked if they could invite families who would appreciate a little assistance. The crew filmed the audience arriving with each person telling Santa what they wanted for Christmas, which was heard by the online retailer's elves (staff). The warehouse went into action, picking the gifts, wrapping them, and getting them into a truck that would drive to the studio. At the finale of the show, the elves appeared giving out the gifts – and everyone got exactly what they asked for!

This story made the news and got media attention from papers and magazines. It also got the ecommerce brand name in front of millions of people nationwide and resulted in an increase in sales that was unprecedented, resulting in the company's best year ever. If I hadn't been alert to the opportunity, then it would never had occurred.

In this chapter we are going to cover:

- What you learnt from your partnership debrief that you can act on straight away.
- How to create a partnership pack that will create a long-lasting impression.
- What area of your communication to target to increase sales.
- How to ramp up your partnership potential so it's on the radar of others, and always have your 'available' taxi light on to make it easy for partners.
- Ultimately, how to take your fifteen seconds of fame and turn it into years of profitability.

TAKE A CRITICAL LOOK AT YOUR LAST PARTNER-SHIP TO FIND THE GAPS AND FILL THEM WITH SALES

Look critically at your last partnership success pack with the metrics, remembering any areas you didn't include due to the results being disappointing. Look at all the elements individually and evaluate them. Creating content is one thing you can always improve, and it's a quick fix, but a low sales conversion rate from shoppers in South Australia may take a little more investigation.

I was an ambassador for LG Electronics and demonstrated their different models of fridges, which were used on their YouTube channel. I thought I did pretty well, until I realised I moved my head to the side and spoke too slowly. I was also a guest on a podcast and really enjoyed the experience. But when I listened to the recording, I realised I had overused the word 'absolutely'.

I once worked with an influencer who was a total professional, was highly engaging on video and had great engagement with her audience. I paid her to write an article for my website, and it was so bad I couldn't use it. As a partner, you need to know where your strengths are and equally what you are not good at so you can navigate away from those elements.

Look for the areas in production you could improve on such as lighting, audio and captions. What is the medium you are most comfortable with? Do you love writing but only long format and struggle with short Instagram captions? Perhaps you love speaking, so concentrate on podcasts. If you are confident about how you look and sound, then YouTube.

But mostly, evaluate what content your audience engaged with that you liked creating. Could you create more? If it's difficult, time consuming and you don't enjoy it, then you won't do it.

Be honest with yourself. It may be too early to make big judgement calls if you're starting out, but it's still good to review and look for ways to improve your content. If you feel judgmental about your content or are hypercritical on yourself, then purely rely on your metrics and those of your partner. Please celebrate all the elements where you did really well. Let it fuel you to do more.

Look across all your metrics

Assess if the metrics achieved the goals you set when you started the partnership. Did you increase your email list but not your following on Facebook? You may have been too grandiose or too frugal when you set your goals, but knowing the metrics allows you be more realistic next time. Most of all, your partnership should have achieved an increase for you in some areas and hopefully the largest metric is a sales increase.

If you provided tea bags in a goodie bag for an event and your goal was to get orders and increase your immediate sales, but instead you gained three new retailers, then you still gained. See it as an opportunity to learn. Perhaps the audience was younger than you thought and they're not your demographic. Maybe they might buy the tea for their mum as a gift. There is still an opportunity to market to the attendees and increase your sales, but having the additional retailers will still help you to achieve your goals.

Assess the metrics you achieve each month on your own, then measure that against what you were able to achieve during the partnership promo period. Do this with all the metrics. Try to also assess the intangible gains – did you learn skills from your partner you didn't have before? Or were you introduced to a new wholesaler?

Don't be hypercritical of what was achieved. If you're still on your training wheels, then try to vary your partnership campaigns to find your sweet spot.

Dive into your audience segmentation post-campaign and see if you have appealed to a different type of customer

It's important to know your customer well and with your increased following or sales, if you identify something different, you can be ready to pounce on it. Imagine you were a small business in NSW and you did a deal with a national partner. You may find you got more customers from regional Queensland than any other region.

You can capitalise on this change of customer by testing some focused Facebook ads on the new demographic in regional Queensland. By using a testimonial from a customer in that locality, you can ignite additional sales in that area. Being alert to new customer segments doesn't mean for a second that you drop your core customer to run after the new crowd, it simply means you are watching and adapting, to capitalise on a spike and see if you can make it a recurring pattern.

TURN ON YOUR TAXI LIGHT TO SIGNAL YOU ARE OPEN TO PARTNERSHIPS

Just like a wedding ring wards off unwanted advances, signaling to others you are interested will attract new attention. Start with the easy digital channels and show you are interested in having a conversation.

Some companies don't want to waste their time, so it feels less obtrusive to make an advance to a party who is willing to have an open conversation. Every company has a contact page on their website, and we take the time to list different email addresses to direct enquiries to the right people.

You could tailor a page on your website so it has a partnerships area, signaling that you are familiar and open to approaches. This shows credibility and also promotes who you've worked with. At the bottom, call out – 'If you'd love to put our heads together and create something together, email partnerships@company.com.au' If you've only had one partnership, use the logo of the company and the product or show media you appeared in. Make it clear it was a marketing partnership and it doesn't look like the brand has a *financial* partnership with you.

Next is your email signature – call out brands you've worked with, media brands, trade shows, etc.

Create an IGTV channel called Partner Love or separate highlight reels for each partner. Write about your partnership experience on LinkedIn and make it part of your bio.

CREATE BRAG VALUE FOR YOUR RETAILERS

As we established in chapter seven, retailers are your original partners – your first backers or supporters and you want to bring them along for the ride, so they can ride on your coat-tails and share your credibility with their customers.

Have you ever been into a furniture store and the owner has picked up a magazine to show you the lounge you are looking at is in a celebrity's house? Or a media outlet has identified the lounge as being in the top five picks for 2021? These are props to assist your retailers to sell your product.

It could be you exhibited at a trade show and your lounge won an award for the best new product. Or productreview. com.au. has voted it 5/5?

The aim is to make it as easy as possible for your retailers to sell your product. Showing you are aligning your brand with other brands that have a high recall value and trust makes it easier for the salesperson to point out the features. This is why you should get showcards from magazines, create POS for awards and create articles that retailers can share on their marketing channels.

Also remember this for when you are prospecting to new

retailers or customers. Ensure your company overview talks about your partnership experience. You may feel like an imposter propping up your brand with other logos, but that's not the case at all. It's a game of inches and everyone is looking for an advantage. Having your brand connected with bigger brands will elevate your business by association.

TALK ABOUT WHO YOU'D LOVE TO WORK WITH – YOU NEVER KNOW WHO IS LISTENING

Flattery will get you most places in life. Many people are gracious and mentioning you hold a brand in high esteem may result in them reaching out to you. That's the opening for a great conversation.

I was recently listening to a podcast – *Stop, Collaborate & Listen* – and a guest was talking about her latest partnership. She was asked who she'd love to work with next. The marketing manager was actually listening and reached out to have a conversation. That's the beginning of a beautiful partnership.

As a first step, contact your favourite podcasts and media outlets in your industry and speak to the editor about yourself, your brand and your recent partnerships. Put yourself forward for panels, webinars and speaking opportunities. This can transform your brand into connections with other people.

Be a little brave and bold – name some companies you'd love to work with when you're at industry events, networking nights, having a meeting with your public relations agency or a sales representative from a magazine. Don't be afraid to do a little LinkedIn stalking to see who is connected to someone you'd like to work with.

If this is freaking you out, think of it from another angle. Imagine you received a company brochure and it spoke about brands the company had worked with, would it increase the credibility of the brand for you? If you think it would make you scared to approach the brand and work with them because you are too small, remember this: they are playing the game too, and they started out the same as you but grew in size or exposure because of the choices they made to elevate their brand.

SNAPSHOT

Business is all about learning and growing. If I could, I would change the four Ps of marketing (product, promotion, place and price) to five Ps and extend this to partnerships, as I think it's the greatest way to leverage a small business' resources and funds to accelerate its growth.

Small business can be lonely, and my experience is that sometimes the decision-making is a heavy cross to carry. Partnerships allow you to work with others, learn from them and create something you couldn't do by yourself. The only thing holding you back from creating your first partnership is the confidence of knowing how. Having completed this book, you now know the path to creating valuable partnerships where you can leverage currencies other than cash.

Take every opportunity this book has shown you and I promise it will elevate you above the hundreds of terrible pitches and partners who under-deliver and never get another shot. What I've shown you in this book doesn't need a double degree from university. Mostly, it's about being diligent and doing the small, but important, things most people can't be bothered to do.

So, now you've created your partnership mindset, have you taken your learnings from this book, knowing you can embrace partnerships of all shapes and sizes with a new-found confidence?

Your partnership possibilities are limitless – I know you can do it!

TAKE CONTROL OF YOUR MARKETING

I hope you've enjoyed this book and feel you can put what you've learned into action. It might feel a little tough at first, but I promise, once you have your partnership mindset switched on, every conversation will spur new ideas on how you can collaborate with others.

So many small companies spend money on building a website with an agency to get the SEO benefits, then create broad Facebook ads in the hope of attracting their ideal customer to their site. How do you know if you are overspending on your Facebook ads? Are you wasting your money on your marketing?

If you want to take control of your marketing, do our marketing scorecard. Discover if you could swap – do you have partnership potential? This will increase your ability to do big brand collaborations and stop paying for promotion.

When you're ready to take the next step, I welcome you to go to www.theresetarlinton.com and download the free resources. There is also a closed Facebook group called 'Swap! Marketing Without Money' that you can join and ask questions or find other brands looking to collaborate.

As someone who really enjoys learning, I personally love participating in courses to put ideas into action. For that reason, I have created some online courses to help you create great partnerships yourself that include:

- Knowing your worth – uncovering the assets you're sitting on.
- Pitch that partnership – how to request and respond to partnership opportunities.
- Do the deal – from the deal memo to executing and over-delivering.
- The success pack – Show the campaign success and create a brand advocate.

Each module has a collection of videos, worksheets and templates to guide you through. They are self-paced online, but since I don't want you procrastinating, you can join me in live group sessions to workshop what you've done.

If your customers are small brands and they would value a partnership education, I love nothing more than being in a room sharing what I know and helping people to bust out and grow. I'd welcome the opportunity to speak at your conference, seminar, webinar or on your podcast.

www.theresetarlinton.com/speaker

To finish up, I've created all the marketing terms you need to know to have conversations with agencies, partners and other brands. These are my definitions not the dictionary's, as I want you to really understand what they mean from a marketing mind.

I look forward to seeing you and hearing about your partnership deals you've been able to do. Please connect with me on Linkedin, Instagram, Facebook or through my website.

LinkedIn: www.linkedin.com/in/therese-tarlinton
Instagram & Facebook: @theresetarlinton

Glossary of Terms

Advertisement
When you create images, testimonials, videos or other assets from a partnership and you agree the other brand can use it as a form of advertising their brand. Used in print on a brochure, sign, poster or digitally on their website or social accounts.

Agency
It could be a talent, PR, advertising or media company that you work with directly or your partnership brand has instructed on their behalf.

Ambassador
An influencer who works with a brand on a long-term contract. An ambassador is essentially the face of the brand during a campaign time frame.

Approvals
When you work with a big brand and they have to float it past senior management to get it signed off before it gets sent to relevant people in the company to execute.

Article
A piece of content that has text and images that conveys a message or story.

Asset
Something you own. It's a product of your knowledge, procedures, your owned communication channels, your foot traffic, email list or your ability, such as being a speaker.

ATL media
Stands for 'above the line' media which is radio, billboard or television which distribute a message to a mass audience of people.

Backup
Clearly this is not a marketing term, but if you create amazing content and then you lose it, you will cry and maybe get fired. Take copies and save them onto another cloud, computer or email them to your personal email.

Batching

When a content creator spends time setting up, then it's easier to create many pieces of content at one time that can be scheduled for use over a longer period. If you're doing your make-up and hair, do all your videos. Bad hair days are for podcasts and writing blogs.

Bio

A few lines on your website or social profile to give the reader more details on your story, your brand and who benefits from your product or service.

Blog posts

An article or thought piece of written content that you post on your own website for your target audience to enjoy. It will include back-links to your other articles, links to other brands products, events or stores and includes images to explain or engage the audience.

Brainstorm

When you come up with random ideas with a group of people and together you refine and sort into a few gems that could work. It's fun and you will come up with better ideas and ways to execute than if you did this alone.

Brand

What people say when you're not near them. References the look, feel, experience, quality and market position of your company and its products.

Brief

A document that provides guidelines on creating content. It includes the messages, asset requirements, handles, links to products and other valuable pieces of information for you to do a great job.

BTL media

Stands for 'below the line' media which is social media, content writing, brochures, targeted advertising like Facebook – a vehicle that can distribute a message to a targeted audience that isn't mass like radio or television.

Budget

How much money can be spent on elements to create a campaign.

Call to action (CTA)
When you have an offer and you invite a prospective customer to do something. This could be to subscribe to a podcast, download a case study, join your Facebook group. The result is that you can communicate with that person into the future.

Campaign
A project outline that will have specifics about dates, parties, communication vehicles and CTA.

Celebrity
Someone that people know because they are a fan of their work in movies, music, TV shows or sports.

Client
If you are receiving money, it's the person paying you.

Community
The people who know, like and trust you. It could be a group of people you've put together that follow you and engage with each other. Or it could be a group you are part of.

Content creators
People you know who include your brand and product when they create content. We love these people! Besides driving traffic and increasing your brand, they just make the content more authentic.

Content
Assets created to drive engagement. This includes photos, videos or text for social media platforms.

Contract
An agreement between two or more parties that includes campaign information and the deliverables.

CPC
Stands for 'cost per click'. If you advertise to drive traffic to your website, it's the amount you paid divided by the number of clicks.

Credibility
A quality we all want – to be trusted, convincing and believed in. You can borrow other brands' credibility by being associated with them.

Deadline
The most important word. It's the date you agree and commit to have something done by. A campaign has a time line attached to every element, with each relying on parties to perform and deliver by a date. If you don't, it puts all the other elements under time pressure.

Deal maker
Any kickass person who reaches out and does a partnership deal with another brand.

Deal memo
An agreement that is not legally binding but has documented times, dates, parties, products and elements each party agrees to deliver on.

Deliverables
What you are responsible for producing (photos/video/text) and publishing (blog post, videos, photos).

Disclaimer
A note that tells people information for disclosure. It could be the story has been paid to be written, an affiliate link where the writer will receive monetary compensation if you buy or that stocks are limited.

Distribution
How your message is spread or your products are enabled to be purchased in a wide manner. By definition it means to 'spread the product' throughout the marketplace such that a large number of people can buy it or consume – it like a video.

Email lists
This is a list of email address that you own that you can use to communicate your message by sending those recipients an email.

Engagement
The number of likes, comments, retweets, shares and repins your content receives.

Engagement rate
The number of followers divided by the number of engagements you have on one post or the average of the last ten posts.

Exclusivity

If a brand asks for exclusivity it refers to a category or industry. It means they don't want you to work with a direct competitor of theirs.

Exclusivity period

The amount of time you are prohibited from working with competitors.

Figurehead

This is the face of the company. It's usually the owner, but for a global company it could be the country manager or another person in the senior management group like the financial controller.

Flat-lay

When you lay items out flat and take photos of them. Could be an outfit, or home building mood board that includes taps, tiles and paint colours.

Gallery

A content option where multiple images can be scrolled through on a blog, Instagram or Facebook post.

Giveaway

A competition to get new customers over to your social accounts or website, get them to sign up to your emails or increase your sales. You offer something for free for them to win.

Guest podcasting

When you approach producers who have a podcast with a defined audience and you appear as a guest on their episode. A brilliant way to get a connection with your target audience as it's a long form of content so the customer gets to hear your story in an authentic way and connect with your brand, values, products and understand how this will benefit them. The podcast host gets to use the guest as a drawcard to gain new subscribers or listeners.

GWP

Stands for 'gift with purchase'. A way to entice customers to purchase with a free gift or increase their basket size by having a gift once they spend over the average amount. This can also be a partner's sample product to help promote two brands.

Hashtag

The # sign used on social media. You can attach to a word or term that strings all your status updates together. Or use as broad terms and industries for new people to find you e.g. #interiordesign

Influencer

A person who has a community that trust them. This term usually relates to an influence online – YouTube, Instagram, a podcast or blog.

Keynote

When a speaker is the headline act on stage for the whole audience to see and hear.

KPI

Stands for 'key performance indicator'. This refers to a metric you to show the success of a campaign. Common KPIs include impressions, engagements, video views, clicks, time on site, purchases, downloads etc.

Launch

When you take a new product to market, publish a book, podcast etc. It's a process where you create the landing page, purchasing ability, communications and collateral and invite people to interact with your new product.

Leadership

Being able to inspire others to perform at the highest level and being prepared to do so yourself.

Leverage

To use everything you've built in your company to your maximum advantage. You have things other brands would love to have, use and associate with. Take what you have built and use its strength to gain in other areas you are weaker in.

Licensing deal

This is a contract between two parties (the licensor and licensee) in which the licensor grants the licensee the right to use the brand name, trademark, patented technology or the ability to produce and sell goods owned by the licensor. In basic terms it's an agreement giving a person or company permission to use or to do something.

Market position
It's the process where you establish the image or identity of a brand or product so that consumers perceive it in a certain way, and distinguishes it from other products of competitors.

Measure
The process where you assess the importance, effect or value of something. You can measure clicks, likes, shares, views, but also brand recall, brand perception and brand sentiment too.

Mention
Calling out the name of a brand on social media using the @ symbol.

Metrics
The system you use to measure something. Clicks, likes, shares, views, sales increase, increased cart size, brand recall and it's usually measured against the industry average or your monthly average.

Mind mapping
This is a structured way to capture and organise ideas and information around a central theme. It can include words, concepts or items linked to a central subject using circles or boxes that radiate out of the centre.

Mood board
A visual representation of a campaign. It can include location, materials, people/customer persona, style of photography etc. Think of it as a giant Pinterest board.

Multiply
Increasing the number greatly. If you have 1,000 followers and you partner with a brand with 1,000 followers, you will increase your potential number of readers, viewers or customers.

Mutual customer
A group of people that has the same feeling or do the same thing. It means they are likely to value your product as they are already a customer of another brand.

Mutuality
The sharing of a feeling, action or relationship between two or more brands. The sentiment is reciprocal. It could be a shared value like commitment to sustainability.

Non-competing

When two or more brands do not sell the same product to the same customer in the same industry. They aren't in competition with each other, rather they are complimentary.

Objectives

These are actionable goals that provide the overall direction to a specific campaign. They are specific, measurable, attainable, relevant and time bound. They are performance indicators and usually include sales growth, lead generation, brand awareness, website traffic and conversation.

Offers

This is when a brand offers a free product or service of value that you give in exchange for people completing a call to action. An offer could be a podcast, ebook, membership to a Facebook group, coupon, trial period or any other vehicle that provides information, service or product at no cost to your potential lead.

Organic reach

When you create a post or video that you share with your audience without payment for promotion.

Outsourcing

When a company hires a company or freelancer to be responsible for planned or existing activity that was done internally. Commonly, brands outsource their social media posting, artwork creation, podcast edit and uploads.

Owned assets/channels

Any digital or physical channels that your brand control to reach or communicate with your customers/audience. It is usually described in a contract and means that the brand can use the content on any owned or operated platforms like their website, blog or social channels. It may also extend to their owned retail locations or offices.

Payment for promotion

When you take an asset and spend money on promoting it to your targeted audience through a third party like Facebook, Instagram, YouTube or display ads on websites

Persona
This is a representation of your target customers. Creating user personas involves researching and outlining your ideal customer's goals, pain points, behaviour and demographic information.

Pitch deck
Usually a PowerPoint presentation that has campaign ideas, ambassadors, costings and timings. The ambition of this document is for another brand to want to partner with you.

PR
Creating media releases or targeting specific journalists and publications for a story to get editorial.

Product
A product is an item offered for sale. It could be a physical good, like a candle, or a virtual good, like an online course. In this book, a product is something you own that can be leveraged.

Product placement
When you place your product strategically on a TV program to increase your visibility and use the distribution and credibility of the program to enhance the perception of your product and the opportunity to increase the sales.

Publicist
This is the person in charge of your public relations. The job is to deal with press, find opportunities for you to extend your brand to give positive reinforcement. This person would also handle damage control if there is a mistake or a scandal.

Public speaking
Traditionally it means the talent of effectively speaking face to face to a live audience. Now it can include a pre-recorded speech, a webinar or a podcast.

Qualitative research
Data collection and analysis using firsthand observations, interviews and questionnaires, focus groups, recordings made in a natural setting or using documents. The data is generally non-numerical.

Reach
The estimated number of potential customers who could see your specific campaign or advertisement.

Resources
What you have to work with. This is your budget, staff, materials, data, technology and digital assets. It can also include physical locations, warehouses and your network you can draw on for assistance.

Retail
Really means a physical location. If a brand or advertiser uses this term it means they want to put the assets you collaborated on together up in the store as a poster or highlight the product you were promoting. It can also mean a reseller of your product that deals with the end consumer if you are a manufacturer.

Reverse brief
Otherwise referred to as the GOLD STANDARD. It's when the brand creates a brief and the other party takes the brief and replies to it, illustrating they understand and can implement by showing them examples of mood boards, images, posts, articles with a tone etc. to reinforce to the brand they will implement to a high standard.

ROI
Stands for 'return on investment'. When a brand spends $1 and gets back $2 the ROI is 2:1. It's the money that is invested divided by the sales they have made.

Sampling
When you offer free product samples or it might be a free period of a service to get new customers. It's used to promote your brand but mostly about product awareness and trialling.

Seeding
Content seeding is a marketing strategy that allows creators to include links to other brands' content across platforms. It could be to promote a product or service, to increase your brand awareness or generate leads with a really compelling CTA (or offer). It's a good test to see if an audience responds before you move into a partnership or pay for advertising.

Sentiment

This is how someone feels after reading your content or buying your product – are they happy, outraged and moved into action, or feel like they've been given false and misleading information? If positive, they can write reviews, give you a five-star rating, talk about your product to their friends or communicate on social media.

Share drive

The location of assets that have been created. It would be a working sheet in the beginning, a place for brand logos, scripts and then content that has been created. Usually done on a Google Drive or Dropbox.

Sharing links

Giving specific users access to digital documents or online content. It also the act of creating content and sharing another brand's assets by including a link to their website or store.

Social media

Any online owned pages on channels you have including LinkedIn, Facebook, Instagram, TikTok, Snapchat etc.

SOW

Stands for 'scope of work' or sometimes 'statement of work'. It outlines exactly what you are hired or expected to do, the budget and the time frames for delivery.

Sponsorship

Where a brand advertiser pays to have both ads and content with their name placed on all materials to do with an event or show, organisation, business or an activity. It's primarily a branding exercise.

Tactics

These are the methods used to achieve a strategy. The detailed actions on how, where and what to promote about a product or service to influence specific marketing goals.

Tag

When you create organic content and you want a brand included. It is the same as a mention but it's a gift not an expectation.

Toolkit

A brand toolkit includes a style guide on how to use the logo, a shared library of logos and images of the product and lifestyle use, copy about the language to use when speaking to the customer and the benefits of the product. It's everything you need to share with a partner to help them create a product that meets your branding expectations and provides clarity to the customers.

Trademarks

An easily recognised symbol, phrase or words legally registered by a company or a product.

Trends

Changes and developments in the market. What the majority of people are being drawn to right now that is changing their behaviour.

Tutorial

Mostly done on YouTube but any video or instructional content where you teach your audience how to do something.

Update

Such an easy thing to do and something not many do. Some campaigns extend over a long period of time and involve many people. Getting into the habit of creating a monthly email that tells your partners what you are doing for them and what else is happening keeps them involved and engaged and loving you to death. Common courtesy and manners are in short supply.

Usage rights

How the content created for a campaign will be used and where it is allowed to appear during a specified time frame.

Vertical

Refers to a category within an industry like style, beauty, fitness, travel, home decor, DIY etc.

Video

To record or broadcast moving visual images. The most engaging form of content that delivers clarity around your brand and your product in an easily consumable way by your target audience.

Webinar

A seminar or digital form of a physical event where one or more speakers meet and give or discuss information, train or demonstrate that is delivered online using webinar software.

Website

A single domain name you type into Google that produces information about your product or brand on pages that is owned and published by you and contains pictures, video, worksheets, blogs or podcast links.

Wrap up

The document you produce to give back to the brand/influencer/agency once you have delivered on your deal to show them what you created and the ROI of this. For example, brand gave $10,000 worth of product and influencer got $50,000 worth of engagement on social and media coverage. The ROI is 5:1 – as the brand invested $10 and got back $50.

YouTube

An online video sharing website where you upload a video. It's a valuable search engine for your brand's content too.

Printed in Australia
AUHW020356230522
363974AU00013B/13